CW00796795

Just a Simple Life...?

Joan Smee

Publishing partner: Paragon Publishing, Rothersthorpe
First published 2017
© Joan Smee 2017

The rights of Joan Smee to be identified as the author of this
work have been asserted by her in accordance with the Copyright,
Designs and Patents Act of 1988.

All rights reserved; no part of this publication may be reproduced,
stored in a retrieval system, or transmitted in any form or by any
means, electronic, mechanical, photocopying, recording or otherwise without the prior written consent of the publisher or a licence
permitting copying in the UK issued by the Copyright Licensing
Agency Ltd. www.cla.co.uk

ISBN 978-1-78222-497-6

Book design, layout and production management by Into Print
www.intoprint.net
+44 (0)1604 832149

Printed and bound in UK and USA by Lightning Source

CONTENTS

Prologue

It was night time and I was lying in bed feeling very scared and anxious. I was alone in the house with my brother Peter. We were very young and our parents were not at home. In those days people didn't lock their doors at night; there was no need to lock doors because people were more trusting then. I was constantly worried at night because at one time someone had been in our house and had stolen a few items of clothing and other things. They had just come in and taken what they wanted and we later noticed things were missing. We also had a small house fire and so there was always that worry for me as well.

I was usually too frightened to close my eyes and I listened out for every creak or unfamiliar sound. In the back garden was a big dark tree which cast sinister moving shadows across my bedroom walls and ceiling. Laying alone in the dark I sometimes had a feeling that there was someone in the room with me. I was frightened of the dark but I remember not feeling at all frightened that there was a presence with me.

I lay there thinking about my family, my home and what my future life would hold. One particular night I had said my prayers and as I tried to fall asleep I had the amazing feeling that I was flying. Although I was lying flat on my bed I was soaring through the air, high up in the sky; it was such a wonderful feeling. I felt very calm; I was light and free and it felt so natural to me. As I was enjoying the flying sensation I could see I was hovering over small dots of coloured lights. When I zoomed in nearer I could see that they weren't lights at all but hundreds and thousands of crystals in every colour imaginable. The crystals seemed alive; they were pulsating and sparkling as they shone out, beckoning me to draw closer. They were absolutely amazing.

I know now that it was a sign to show me that I would live with colour for the rest of my life – and I have done. To me colour is life and the spectrum of colour is huge.

Why were Peter and I left alone in the house at such a young age though?

I would like to dedicate this book to my wonderful family for their infinite love and support, for being on this journey with me and for patiently listening to my story so many times for most of their lives.

1

Growing up in the 30s

My earliest memory of life was being with my dad. I was always a weak child and I suffered with chronic bronchitis. In those days bronchitis was a serious illness. Daddy made up a small bed for me downstairs in the living room. He stoked up the fire to keep me cosy, made me warm drinks and fed me soup. He was so kind and gentle and he did everything for me; I loved my daddy and I know he loved me.

I was born in 1930 and my brother, Peter, in 1929. We were both born in Lincoln in the industrial north of England. My mum and dad were Ivy and Harold Thomas. They were both the same age and when they met, dad was living in lodgings in the next street. Mum was born in Norfolk and dad in Wales. They both played the piano and often performed duets together in the local pubs and clubs, dressed in their matching brown suits. My dad worked at the John Lysaght steelworks, and later at Appleby and Frodingham in Scunthorpe. I never met my dad's family but I was told that his father's name was Moses. I believe that my ancestors could have been immigrants from somewhere in Europe. At that time there was no work in their home country so they emigrated and managed to settle in Wales because there was work available in the Port Talbot area. When the family was asked their surname they said it was 'Thomas' because there were thousands of people with the name of Thomas in Wales and that surname fitted in. So that was my father's family and is as much as I know of them.

One evening when I was about four years old mummy and daddy had supper together. Everything seemed normal and I was tucked up in bed.

7

Early the next morning I woke up, got dressed and went downstairs for breakfast. I thought it was unusual that the fire was not made because daddy always started the fire in the mornings before he went off to work. We had a brass fender in the fire grate with two small box-seats on either side where all the boot polish and brushes were kept. I was sitting on one of these seats and my brother Peter came in and said to me

'Where's daddy?' I didn't know where he was. I could hear Peter's voice shout upstairs

'Mum, daddy's not here and there is no fire but his sandwich box is still here.'

'Perhaps he was late this morning. Are his shoes there?'

'Yes, they are.'

'I will get up and come down and make the fire,' mum answered.

Mummy came down with her Teddy Bear coat on over her nightdress. The coal house was outside and so was the toilet; the kitchen was just like a small scullery. We always kept a bucket of coal and some firewood indoors. Mummy started laying the fire and I had a strong feeling that she was going to go into the kitchen next. I was thinking 'Mummy's going to get the wood' and I don't know why but I felt compelled to walk in front of her into the kitchen. I opened the kitchen door and there was my daddy lying on the floor behind the door. I almost fell over him! His head was laid on the bottom shelf of the gas oven. I remember thinking how yellow he looked. The smell of gas was terrible and made me cough.

Mummy followed me into the kitchen. She saw daddy and she quickly snatched me back out of the kitchen and slammed the door shut. I was just four years old. It was an enormous shock to me. I remember panicking and shouting

'What's the matter with daddy, what's the matter with daddy? Why does he look so yellow?'

Mummy started screaming and ran outside. When she came back she was accompanied by a policeman.

Throughout that day many people came in and out of the house. While all this was happening I didn't cry. I just felt numb and bewildered and I didn't quite understand what was happening. I was so young. I didn't know what suicide was; nobody explained anything at all to me. Mum never sat me on her knee and talked to me about things but then she had disowned me at birth. That is why my dad was the one who looked after me. I knew straight away that daddy's was the only love I was ever going to get. He was gone forever and I knew that mummy didn't love me. I sensed that, even at that young age. Mummy loved Peter; he was her first born and in her eyes Peter couldn't do anything wrong; she didn't love me.

A man from the steelworks came to give his condolences to mummy and they were sitting together talking. I knew she was talking about daddy and I suddenly started crying, thinking 'Where is my daddy? They are talking about him.' I became very upset and I put my face on mum's shoulder. She rebuffed me and pushed me away saying

'Now look what you have done! Look at the mess your tears have made on my dress.'

She must have felt sorry afterwards because she gave me some sweets. Was she really sorry, or did she do that because we had a visitor?

On the day of the funeral mummy said

'You had better go into the front room and give your daddy a kiss because you won't see him again.'

I went into the room where daddy was lying in his coffin. I came up to about mum's waist and the top of the open coffin was higher than that. The coffin was placed on a trestle and the legs stuck out so I tried to climb up one of the legs. I just managed to peep over the top. Daddy was dressed all in white with lace tucked around him. He didn't look as yellow then; he just looked as if he was asleep; he looked very peaceful. I didn't feel frightened at all seeing him there, I just felt very sad and empty, just as if a big part of me was missing. I tried my hardest to reach over and kiss daddy but I couldn't, I was too small. So I kissed my hand and placed it on his cheek, which I could just about reach. He felt icy cold. Then I started crying and I just couldn't stop. I was missing him so much already. I knew, without anyone telling me, that from then on life was going to be very lonely for me. I was wise even at that age. That was the end of the only parent and relative who loved me.

A funeral was held for daddy but I don't remember being taken to it. I just knew that was the day my daddy was going away from me forever. No one in the family talked to me or explained what had happened or about life and death or where daddy went to. My dad just disappeared from my life! It wasn't until many years later, through a psychic reading, that I learned more about why my daddy had to leave us.

❧

One day, some time after my dad had died, my mum went on holiday with Peter, locked the house up and left me in my bedroom. After a while I began to cry. The neighbours were outside talking and they could hear a child crying but they didn't know where the noise was coming from. My crying had been going on for some time and one of the women managed to get into the house and found me in my bed, sitting on a soaked mattress in my own urine and mess, and of course I hadn't been fed! I think mum was hoping that I would have died while she and her darling son Peter were away. A kindly neighbour took me back to her house and looked after me.

The lady who took me to her home was called Mona White and she must have looked after me for quite some time. I don't remember too much of that part of my life but I do remember that Mona was always kind to me. I remember quite vividly the day Mona returned me to my mum and my strong feeling that mummy didn't want me or love me. It was a bad and heavy feeling. Mum was sitting curling her hair and getting ready for work. I could hear Mona saying

'Well Mrs Thomas, I can't have Joanie any more. I have my own commitments and I cannot afford to keep her so I have brought her back to you.'

Mona left and mum said to me

'Oh, so I have got you back have I?'

I knew my mummy didn't want me back. It seemed she couldn't bear to touch, hug or kiss me. Several weeks later I was due to start school aged five.

Mona White wasn't a close neighbour; she lived on the other side of the road to us. I can remember the people who did live next door to us. We lived near the High Street and the lady next door was called Bridget. When I was older another neighbour used to ask me to take a jug full of tea down to her sister who worked at the Laundry shop in the High Street. People took in their dirty laundry and when it was washed it was folded neatly and tied up in brown paper with string around it. Bridget used to give me sixpence for doing that and I spent the money on fabric to make patchworks. I loved different fabrics and was attracted to the colour and feel of them even at that young age. Bridget told people what a darling little girl I was.

From then on in my life I did everything for myself. Mum earned her living playing the piano in the local working men's clubs and pubs. In those days the working men's clubs were very popular and were a big part of the social scene. They were everywhere in the north of England. The only time mum was nice to me was when she came home with a lot of people from the clubs or if she had been drinking. It seemed as if mum was always out.

Scunthorpe was a large industrial city and in those days nearly every other door belonged to a pub. When my mum was 17 her mum used to say 'Come on Ivy, get yourself ready, we are going out.' Mum never knew where they were going. Nan used to take mum into the clubs and pubs and they spent most of the night in the club singing and with mum playing the piano. In the pub nan said 'Come on Ivy, get up and play.'

My mum could play the piano very well and most of the people sang along with her. She was given free drinks all night even though she was only 17 years old. For nan it just meant free entertainment and free drinks, so it was a good evening out for her. Mum just accepted it and didn't seem to resent her mother for encouraging her to play, even though she would have preferred to be able to play the piano professionally. She tolerated it because she was well treated. Mum was everyone's friend and often played at their private parties.

Grandparents: Charlie and Lydia Tuck.

My mum's side of the family was quite large and they were talented musically. There was my nan, Lydia Tuck and granddad Charlie Tuck. They had four daughters: Ivy, Florence, Violet and Sylvia. Florence died as a child. Auntie Sylvie was around 12 years younger than mum and she featured a lot in my early life. There was also auntie Violet and her husband, Uncle Bill, who died of cancer. Uncle Bill crouched right down to me – and he had a really deep voice; he looked at my face and hugged me in my tummy.

'Who's going to giggle for me then?' he said, because I was a little giggler and I had a really infectious laugh. I loved him, I really did. I didn't see him very often but when I did he held out a coin to me and said

'Come on, I have got this for you if you come and giggle for me.' He gave me half a crown.

Peter and I were always polite and well-behaved. I never sat down until I was told to and so I never caused my mum any problems. I could never understand why she didn't like me. It was probably just the fact that she didn't want the responsibility; she could cope with one child but not with two. She didn't want children hindering her life. Also Peter weighed nine pounds when he was born. I weighed six pounds and was a forceps delivery; maybe that was another reason why mum never liked me: because my birth was more difficult for her.

As I was growing up I had several friends but I never knew whether mum was upstairs in bed or out in the clubs playing the piano. A lot of the time she didn't come home all night. Peter and I were left to fend for ourselves with no adult in the house. In the mornings we had to get ourselves ready for school and I cleaned the house for mum before I went to school. I was only in the Infants school but strangely I used to feel sorry for her and I always wanted to please her. As time went on I think mum must have had money worries because sometimes when I returned home from school I would look around in the bedrooms and they would look different. I gradually realised that pieces of furniture were missing, a dressing table or chest of drawers. I didn't understand what was happening then but now I look back I believe she may have had to sell things in order to pay the bills or buy food. Eventually all that was left in my bedroom was an iron bed and mattress and it was always cold in there. Mum had her wages from playing the piano in the clubs but she couldn't have earned much from that and she had rent to pay plus two children to support on her own. I did feel sorry for her and I still do, it must have been a very difficult time for her.

When I was older mum sometimes took me to the clubs with her and I was occasionally given money by one of her friends. Mum was known as 'Our Ivy'. Everyone loved Ivy and enjoyed listening to her play the piano so she soon forgot about her two young children alone at home. It was quite a lonely life, without a dad and never knowing when you would next see your mum. I could draw and when I was alone I picked up my paper and pencils and drew anything I could. No one in my family actually taught me or showed me how to draw but I loved it. I saw pictures in the newspaper and copied them; I loved faces and drew those I especially liked. If I liked clothes and fashion, then I copied those too.

Although mum played the piano well she never taught me to play, which was sad really. Sometimes she asked me to sing in the clubs. I loved singing and I still do. My grandmother had a real strong contralto voice. We had so many musical instruments in the house. Granddad played the euphonium, that's the big brass instrument. My auntie Sylvie sat at one end of the piano and mum sat at the other end. They got through a whole music book on a Sunday afternoon and then they played all the songs which they could harmonise together on.

My nan went to the under-stairs cupboard and got out her piano harp and played along with them. Nan sang along as well and her voice boomed out; she certainly knew how to sing. She was a very cultured lady. She sometimes played a big piano accordion and the family all played their instruments together. Nan also had a lovely, tiny push-button squeeze box. Not one of my family taught me to play but auntie Sylvie, after she was married and had her first child, one day said 'Come on, let's have a duet. I want you to play.' It was magical and I loved those times. Auntie Violet couldn't play anything musical but she was a wonderful writer. She won competitions for her writing. My family were all very talented people.

Sometimes auntie Sylvie came into the house with the band and they had a jam session. She played the piano; she could play almost anything. She would hear a song on the radio, and she would play along. My mum could read music and played a church organ as a child of 11. My granddad told her to learn to play so that she could play to the church congregation on a Sunday. She had to learn to play hymns and that was a big task for her. She practised every night after school. Auntie Sylvie said

'Your mum would be tearing her hair out trying to pull out all the organ stops and work the foot pedals.'

She was a genius really and I think about how all that is in my family and in my own blood.

I had several spiritual experiences throughout my early life. I knew my nan was psychic and I knew my mum was too. Mum used to say

'I can see your dad, he is in the room.'

I didn't really understand it then and she never tried to educate me further about it. I was never frightened of it and it just seemed normal in our family. I don't understand why nothing was ever explained to me. It was as though I didn't quite belong to the family. I often wondered if I was really my mum's child.

Harold and Ivy Thomas with baby Peter.

15

2

Coping as children home alone

I was a tomboy when I was a kid. My friends used to say 'Let's go and knock the door and ask if we can take the baby for a walk.' I always wanted to climb trees, not take babies out!

As a young child my nan didn't treat me badly but she didn't do anything for me either. My granddad used to give me sixpence pocket money each week and I usually spent it on small pieces of material and colourful patchwork squares. Collecting fabric and material was my hobby as a child and it still is.

My first day at school was not a very good experience for me. As small as I was at that age, no one walked me to school. I did know where the school was though. On my first day I asked my teacher if I could go to the toilet. Just as I went to step inside the cubicle, someone pushed me from behind with such a force that I fell and hit my face on the toilet. I had blood all over me and when the teacher saw me coming back she ran outside, took me to the cloakroom and laid me on the floor.

Later in the day I still had to walk home on my own. My face had swollen up and my head hurt. When I got home my mother was eating her meal and I put my head on her lap and cried and cried. Why would someone do such a horrible thing to me?

Most nights Peter and I were left in the house on our own. I had to put myself to bed and get myself up in the morning for school. I was sometimes told, in front of the class,

'Get to the cloakroom Joan and wash your hands, they are disgusting!'

Before I went to school I always made a fire for mum, just like my

16

dad had done every morning. I didn't look at my hands; you don't when you are a kid. My hands were dirty and my hair was matted; I couldn't get a comb through it. I must have looked a sight but that is just how my life was then.

I was pushed into the local swimming pool when I was young – and I couldn't swim! After that I decided I had to learn to swim and I went to the pool every night after school and taught myself to swim. I watched the other kids playing in the water. Swimming meant everything to me at that time, I just loved it. I learnt to dive and I was chosen to represent the school for diving. I became quite a champion swimmer and received certificates and trophies for it. I went swimming on Saturdays and stayed there all day. There were no time restrictions like there are now.

After swimming I was always starving so I walked to the fish and chip shop on the way home for four pence worth of chips with scraps and salt and vinegar. Scraps were the bits of fish and batter at the bottom of the tray. It was the best meal I could have had because the chips were hot and the smell of the vinegar was just the best. I walked home eating these as I went, feeling quite content. For me those were some of the good days.

My mother never came to school to see me in any plays or swimming galas, or to view my art displays or anything else I made. My art was on display around the school. When I made anything I was always top for crafts; anything arty, I excelled at. Mum never wanted to buy anything which belonged to me and I could never understand my aunties or my nan never buying or showing an interest in any of my work. I have been quite successful in a lot of things throughout my life and it has been my own doing. I got top marks for everything I made at school. I made baskets lined with silk to put cottons in; they were lovely but my family didn't want any of it. They said

'What are we going to do with it?'

All the kids who lived in my part of the High Street met up and played rounders or hide and seek. It was different playing these games outside rather than indoors. All the girls played skipping.

They did fancy step-up skipping which I thought was clever. We had a bicycle wheel and we competed to find out who could run with it fastest. The girls bounced balls against the wall and then bounced them around their body, between the legs and backwards. Then we juggled with two balls.

In the winter when the ice and Jack Frost came, it was freezing cold because Lincolnshire is very flat. We made a slide along the middle of the road and waited our turn to jump on it. The slide became like glass; we took a run-up and onto the slide. It was great fun. Not everyone could do it though. It was a long slide and the air came billowing out of everyone's mouths and looked like steam. The snow covered the whole front doorways; we had to break it down to get out for school. I have never seen snow like it since then.

Peter and I continued to bring ourselves up the best way we could. I remember when I was about seven years old we were both still alone in the house most of the time. Every morning we got ourselves up and went to school and when we arrived home in the afternoon there was still no one at home. We fed ourselves with whatever we could find in the larder. We hadn't seen anyone the night before either so we went to bed on our own. It seemed such a long time to me.

Peter and I played together and had good fun but as he grew older he became quite nasty to me. He realised that my mum didn't like me and he said

'There's something wrong with you because mum doesn't like you.'

When mum came home she had often bought something for him. She never came back with anything for me and he picked up on this, so he treated me with contempt – just as she did. When mum brought him in a comic, The Dandy or Hotspur, and I asked if I could have one too she said

'There's nothing for you, they don't have comics for girls.'

There were comics for girls of course but maybe she thought I was too young for them? Peter was the best in my mother's eyes and he could do no wrong. Peter always appeared resentful of my dad for leaving us.

My best friend, Yvonne, lived near me and I often went to call for her. I knocked the door and her mother opened it and invited me in. She said 'Sit down Joan.' There was a fire ablaze in the grate and the house was all cosy and warm. On the table was a little pack of sandwiches made for Yvonne; they were so neatly wrapped in greaseproof paper. Her mother brushed Yvonne's hair and made her look pretty. I remember thinking how lucky she was to have a mother and home life like that. What I liked about my friend's house was that her mother accepted me the way I looked. My friend became the beauty queen of our town. Mind you I could have won if I had entered and hadn't been taken away from home. *Ha!*

I sometimes played with another friend who once kept a shoe box full of my patchworks and I never forgave her for that. That work had cost me a lot of sixpences to gather and they just fitted into one box. I had several shoe boxes of my work but she always denied having that particular one. I had left it at her house because I was going to go back and play with her later. Her name was Eileen Ramshaw and her family was Irish. She stubbornly denied having the box. I was so hurt to think that one of my friends had done that to me and I felt betrayed for a long time. I promised myself that nobody would ever do that to me again!

At home I gathered all my shoe boxes, took all the patchworks out and I made the most enormous patchwork quilt. Every piece of patchwork was hand-stitched together and for a long time I had a hole in my finger from sewing it because I didn't own a thimble! My auntie Sylvie came in and said

'Who has made this?'

'I have,' I replied

'What, you have stitched that all together yourself?'

'Yes, I have used about four whole cotton reels stitching it.'

Auntie Sylvie was impressed that I had sewed all the squares together myself and had produced a beautiful quilt.

I went into town once with a girl who lived near me. She was older than me and one day she said

'Bring your pram and we will go shopping. You can have anything you want from Woolworth's and it is all free.'

What a treat I thought! So, we walked into Woolworth's and she kept reminding me that everything was free and I must help myself to whatever I wanted. I trusted her, she was older than me after all and I looked up to her. I filled the pram up with lots of nice toys and books and took them home. When my mum saw them all in the pram she went mad.

'What do you think you have been doing?' she screamed at me. I told her it was alright because everything was free. My friend had assured me of that.

Mum did no more than drag us two and the pram straight back to Woolworth's to return the items. We had to apologise to the manager. I clung to a cute little teddy bear and really didn't want to part with him but in the end I had to of course. I was so sorry and bitterly disappointed!

I missed out on some of my schooling because at different times a teacher would take me out of the class and tell me to sit down and draw. Another time I put on a concert and I made all the costumes and organised the routine because I had music and entertainment in my family. Alas, my talents were wasted on my family. If only I had had parents who had been together lovingly and said 'Look our Joan has these talents, let's encourage her and get her trained.' My nan kept saying 'We must get Joan into sewing, into a shop somewhere.' Nothing ever came of that.

I lived near the High Street and on a Saturday after the shops were closed the shopkeepers threw all the items they didn't want away and they were put around the back of the shops in big bins. There was a dress shop where my friend and I rummaged in the dustbins for all the old fabric off-cuts. You could get all sorts of remnants; gold ribbons, silk, lace, etc. One day one of the women workers saw us and asked what we were looking for. I told her we needed off-cuts to make dolls clothes.

'Hang on a minute, I can do better than that.' she said.

She came back with some larger pieces of material for us and I never forgot her for that.

I could have had an apprenticeship there; sat at the table stitching and I could have created my own designs and sold them because I was so interested in fashion. I am not religious but I have always said thank you for what has been given to me and for what I could do because it has always helped me through my life. People were always amazed at my talents but nobody did anything about it.

In the High Street there was a men's tailor shop called Weavers to Wearers (similar to Burtons) and the Cotton Shop. One time I found a beautiful piece of silky orange velvet. It was used for display; it would be placed over the manikin's neck and the man's suit jacket would be placed around it. I was thrilled with that and thought I could make something really good with it.

We also found in the bins behind the shops boxes of display chocolates with wooden dummy sweets in and we played jokes on people with those. The boxes of chocolates were elaborate, with lovely pictures of pretty roses, cute kittens and thatched cottages on them. Then there were wide, colourful silky ribbons tied around the box. They looked lovely.

My mother didn't hate me all of the time. I sometimes watched her in the kitchen making a meal. One day I asked if I could make some food in the kitchen. Mum got several ingredients and utensils out onto the table but instead of showing me what to do she walked out of the kitchen saying

'Right, get on with it then.'

I mixed all the ingredients together and made a cake – of sorts!

3

War children on the move

The Second World War started in 1939 and Peter and I were still being left on our own. I was nine and Peter was 11 years old. All the windows and doors in the house had to be blacked out. No light was allowed to show at all. If we went outside and through one door, we had to make sure that the next door was closed first so that no light was visible. There were never any street lights on and everywhere was so dark with just the moonlight showing on clear nights. I went to the cinema sometimes, just to be with company and to feel safe. When we came out of the cinema I ran home as fast as I could and raced indoors.

One night Peter and I had made a fire in the grate because we were cold and it also gave us some light to see with. Peter kept bullying me to go outside and get some more coal in. He wouldn't go and get it and I said

'No, I won't go, I am too frightened.'

I was crying and scared and I told him to fetch the coal himself because he was bigger than me. It was complete darkness outside and in the back garden there was a big tree which made the house really dark inside as well. Peter kept harassing and bullying me to go, so in the end I did. I didn't like him for the way he bossed me about. He told tales about me to mum and then she told me off. I felt so very alone at times.

We were told that if we heard bombs dropping and a whistle blowing we had to drag the table to the corner of the room where the stairs were because the stairs often remained standing when a house or building was bombed. So that was exactly what we did

– and it meant survival for us! We picked up the heavy scrub-top table and carried and dragged it into the corner as best we could. We gathered up the big velvet cushions from the three-piece suite and placed them under the table. We had a thick, red velvet cord-type tablecloth over us as a cover and we went to sleep like that. We were lying there alone and scared but the tablecloth felt comforting somehow. We went to sleep wondering if our house would be bombed next or even whether we would wake up the next morning.

When we did wake up we got ourselves up and ready for school. No one came to see if we were alright – or even if we were still alive! I always felt anxious and I wet the bed sometimes because the toilet was outside and I was so frightened to go out into the dark.

When I arrived at school the following day I heard people saying that a house had been hit and one of the mothers was hurt by a falling drainpipe and masonry. I felt sure it was my entire fault because I had been outside getting the coal in and maybe I had left a chink of light for the enemy. I lived with that guilt for a long time but I didn't dare tell anyone about it.

We often heard planes flying over the school and air-raid sirens blaring followed by bombing noises. Later in the war we saw a fight in the air between a Spitfire and a Messerschmitt. All the children were being ushered into the air raid shelters and I remember standing there just looking up into the sky fascinated and not quite realising what was happening. There was a lot of smoke in the sky but the teacher shouted at me to get into the shelter. Sometimes it was too late to get into the air raid shelter so we went into the school hall. We usually sat on the floor. If that happened the teachers didn't carry on with lessons; the piano teacher played and we all sang songs – to lessen the fear no doubt.

When I was nine or 10 years old, I got scabies, which is a contagious skin condition caused by tiny mites that burrow into the skin. The mites apparently came over from foreign countries on the cargo contained in boats and they clung onto anything they could. They were carried from person to person via newspapers and clothing. The main symptom of scabies is the intense itching and it is worse at night when the environment is warm. The scratching causes a skin rash on areas where mites have burrowed. I could feel them crawling around under my skin. It was awful and I was horrified when I found out what was wrong with me; but of course I had no family to check on my health so I had to go to the clinic on my own. My mum was never in the house for me to talk to her about it; I was always on my own, apart from Peter. We wore the same clothes every day so it is no wonder the mites felt at home on me! We had no bathroom and only cold water to wash in.

Scabies became an epidemic in parts of the country during war-time. So many people suffered with it but if it was identified early it was treatable. I became lousy with it and had no idea what was wrong with me. The treatment for scabies then was Calamine Lotion. You had to paint it on your body, have a daily bath and put on clean clothes every day. That was virtually impossible for me at that age. I just couldn't keep still because I was constantly itching. It was dreadful and I felt so unclean.

I was sitting eating my tea and for once my mum was sitting beside me and Peter was on the other side, which was a rare occurrence. Mum could see me wriggling and scratching and she told me off saying

'For God's sake stop scratching and keep still will you!'

I looked down and started crying because she had told me off. She never said 'What's wrong darling?' I wasn't scratching on purpose, I just couldn't stop it. I could feel the mites constantly moving around all over my body. She told me off again and I couldn't eat my tea because I was so distressed. She didn't explain what was wrong with me; I don't think she had it in her to help me. She said

'I will look at you when we have finished tea.'

We eventually finished eating and she said

'Come here!'

She lifted up my top and said

'Oh my God! You have got spots all over you. It's the clinic for you tomorrow!'

The next day I had to go to school first then I told the headmistress that my mum said I had to go to the clinic because I had spots all over me. I always had to go to the clinic on my own; mum never came with me.

I must have had scabies for some time because they spread to Peter. He was the only other person in the house and we didn't have a bathroom. Once I had started applying the Calamine Lotion the scabies disappeared. As a child, something like that seems like a mountain in your head and was something I had to face alone. There was no one to comfort me. My granddad was the only person in my family who showed me any kindness. When I stayed with my grandparents, granddad made me breakfast. He lifted his walking stick up and prodded the ceiling of the bedroom so I knew my breakfast was ready. There were fried potatoes, bread and butter and a mug of tea.

Another night the sirens went off and that meant there were German planes flying over Scunthorpe, searching for the steelworks to drop their bombs on. We heard the whizz and roar of the bombs and then loud bangs and other dreadful crashing noises. The noise was so loud and the house shook and shuddered because we lived quite near the steelworks.

Eventually our house did suffer from bomb damage and it was condemned as unfit to live in. All the wallpaper kept falling off the walls and they had a white sort of 'frost' growing on them. I couldn't understand why the bricks were growing a glistening white 'frost'. It was all over one particular wall and it was bad for us, living in such a damp house. I had suffered from bronchitis when I was younger as well. We had no hot water and the cold tap was outside along with the toilet and coal house. Only the sink and the gas cooker, which had a very low door and a big, thick handle, were inside. There was a pantry where we used to make our sandwiches. We went back out to play with a great big doorstep-sandwich in our hands, and everybody wanted one. We didn't dare give food away though because it was hard to come by then and food was strictly rationed.

The house became uninhabitable and mum was told that we had

to leave and find somewhere else to live. At that time we had a lovely Dalmatian dog called Trixie. She had just had a litter of puppies and they were really gorgeous. Trixie was a good guard dog and barked as soon as anyone came near Peter or me. When we had to move out of the house mum had to get rid of the dog, which was awful because she was like a best friend to me. Peter and I used to dress Trixie up in mum's best clothes and later put them back in the wardrobe, hoping that she would never notice they had been disturbed in any way. We loved that dog!

When we moved house, Trixie just disappeared and I was never told what had happened to her. It was only several years later, when Peter and I met up again, that I discovered Trixie had gone to live on a farm as a working dog. I missed her terribly and had often wondered where she had gone.

When we moved to the next house I met a girl there who was more or less the same age as me. We only lived there for a short time though because my mum and Vera, the lady who owned the house, clashed. I think Vera lived with the lodger and mum didn't approve. After that we ended up living with my nan and granddad and it was awful living there because everybody dictated to me. It was always me who was the cause of arguments because auntie Sylvie used to say

'Joan, I am not telling you again, do this or do that.'

'Yes, auntie Sylvie.'

I did whatever was asked. Then my mother turned around and said

'Oh that's alright, I am only your mother and you do what she wants you to do. When I tell you to do something you will do it!'

I was always torn between the two of them. My nan was a Victorian woman and was very strict with her girls and they were very stern with me.

One time I was called a liar because I had made a skirt from an old gymslip that I had. When I was about 11 years old I had joined a group and we had to wear white blouses and a navy blue skirt. My mum didn't even know anything about it; I just asked her if I could cut my old gymslip up to make something and she said

'Yes, if you want to.'

I left the pocket on but took the two straps off and I put the darts in myself.

The lady in charge said

'Well, one or two of you have tried to make an effort but Joan has made her own outfit. Come on Joan, stand up and show us.'

One of the girls called out

'She's a liar. She didn't make it herself, her mother made it for her.'

The girl couldn't believe that I had actually made something myself. No one showed me how to sew, I just picked it up.

I sometimes made things like scarves and mittens for the war effort and gave them to mum to be raffled off at the clubs. She said to me

'You have been given a few shillings for that pair of mittens you made.'

I cut anything up – blazers, skirts and clothes – that had not been used for a long time. I embroidered them as well. Mum was civil in that way; she usually let me have the material. I even had my name in the local paper for my work, for helping with the war effort. I was into everything like that because I was left on my own such a lot and so I learnt to do all those things.

While I was still of school age we sometimes went and worked in the fields in the holidays. The farmer said

'Is there anyone who would like to come and work on the farm and help do the harvesting?'

This was in August and my arm used to shoot up so that I could earn some money to give to my mum.

I had a good singing voice and I was asked to sing. I loved singing. I used to sing in the fields with two little Irish girls, Joy and Irene. We all sang while we were picking spuds, covered with mud all over. I loved those days, I loved the companionship. I was never dressed properly for working in the fields. I got bleeding legs, really badly bleeding, like razor blade cuts and in the heat they split open and bled.

My mum never ever did anything about them and she didn't even mellow as she got older. I always felt duty-bound to bring in some money for mum. There was a lot of unhappiness at home and dictatorship and rows. My auntie Sylvie was an absolute spitfire at times and she would really lay into me if she was having an argument with my mum.

Near to where I lived and just around the corner into the High Street there was a laundry shop. Next door to that was a sweet shop and tobacconist. I went in there for some sweets when they had any in stock. The war was still on and sweets were hard to come by. I am sure that people could smell sweets because they all seemed to know when they were in and there was always a queue. I got to know the lady who owned the shop. She was always on her own in there. She let me go behind the counter and break boxes up to flatten them and tidy up for her. I rather liked it. She showed me how to use the scales and how to dress the window. It did help that I was 'arty'.

She had another shop which I hadn't been to and which was at the bottom of the High Street but right alongside of the bus station. She asked me if I would mind looking after the shop as there was no one to run it. It would only be for a short time. I just nodded my head. I was a bit worried about the money side of it as I was not very good at maths at school. Anyway, I went in for a few days and the queue of people came and went. I could get rid of a shop full. The customers used to say

'Ay, she's a keen one that little'un. She has the shop sorted out like nobody's business.'

There was a piano shop opposite the sweet shop and the man from there came in for his 20 Kensitas cigarettes; sometimes he bought 40. He put the money on the counter and I gave him his change. He always said to me

'I tell you what, heads I win and tails you lose.'

That meant that I always lost and I fell for it every time! It was only coppers but we used to laugh about it. I liked the work but I didn't like the lady who owned the shop; she was rather strange. There would be a queue in and out of the shop after an allocation of sweets. For some time after the war shops only had a limited allowance of goods. You couldn't get sweets or tobacco very often. People seemed to somehow know when a delivery was about to come in because when that happened it was busy all day in the shop. The owner came back and did all the cashing up at the end of the day. I don't remember if she paid me or not – the mean bugger.

One day I was making room for some new stock that had just come in. I looked to see what was in one bag from the old stock. It was Turkish Delight. I thought it must have been there for ages and no one would notice if I took one piece to try. I ate just one piece and it tasted just 'delightful'.

I carried on taking the new stock in. The man who was delivering it all in was so quick I didn't know what to do with it all. Later on, the lady shop owner came in; she looked around and tapped on a box. She looked at the bag of Turkish Delight and put it straight onto the scales. She looked at the weight and said

'Have you had some of this because it is for a customer?'

I was honest and told her that I had one piece – I couldn't say anything else. I didn't realise it was for a customer and I felt very guilty and was sorry. I didn't go back to the shop again. That was another of life's lessons for me.

I remember the prisoners of war. My uncle was in charge of Polish, Czech, Germans and Yugoslavs in a big camp somewhere on the outskirts of Scunthorpe. One time I saw the Italians walking along the road with big yellow patches on their coats. I was as tall as them and I was about 13; I thought how small the Italian men were.

As the war years progressed I still continued to work on the farm in the holidays. I managed to get the workmen's bus which took me almost there. It was bitterly cold and I only had a jacket on and a pair of my brother's trousers which fitted me better than they did him. He would have complained if he had seen me wearing them but clothes were rationed then so we had to make do. It was a fair walk once I was off the bus so I put my head down and got on with it. When I knocked on the farmhouse door, the farmer's wife was surprised to see me because the other pickers didn't turn up in the bad weather.

There was a roaring fire in the lovely big kitchen and a large scrub-top table. It felt warm and comfortable, not like my cold house with its cold water tap, no hot water, outside toilet or bathroom. The farmer's wife had a piece of fish frying on the fire. She told me to sit down and she put the fish on a plate in front of me. Wow! I had never seen such a big plateful. It was sizzling in its wonderful golden brown, crispy batter just like from the 'Chippie'. The farmer's wife said

'Work in the top field today.'

So off I went and when I got there I was shocked because I found several prisoners of war working on the field. I just stood there, staring and not knowing what to do. I didn't look at them and I quickly started picking the potatoes. The potatoes had clay on them which made them weigh heavy in the basket.

One day a big German prisoner-of-war picked me up and placed me on top of the potato pile, much to the amusement of the other men. The German was a big man and like a giant next to me; I had to look up to talk to him. When my basket was full of potatoes he ran up to me, picked up the basket and took it to the end of the field, to what was called a 'pie'. The 'pie' was a huge pile of potatoes which had clay all around it and a roof on top for protection. The potatoes were muddy and piled up with clay all around them and this apparently protected them.

The German POW carried my basket to the pie several times. I thanked him but knew I couldn't fraternise with the enemy, it was unpatriotic. I saw a German man who looked to be about 16 years old and I thought to myself that he was very young to be a prisoner. While we were working, it started to rain so the big German took off his coat and placed it around my shoulders. He then tied the coat up with string to keep it from falling off me. I was a midget in those days and the coat was miles too big – but it kept me dry and warm and I was grateful for it.

One day when I returned home from working at the farm my mum was actually kind to me. She handed me a small blue envelope addressed to me. The handwriting was the most beautiful, neatly-written gothic writing I had ever seen. I didn't know who could have sent me a letter like that. I opened the envelope and inside was a one-page letter. It was from the younger German man. He said how sweet I had looked sitting on top of the pie and that he couldn't get me out of his mind. He asked me to go out with him. My mum read the letter over my shoulder. He had drawn a misty heart shape with the pencil smudged to make it look softer with an arrow through the heart. His name was Ernst but I didn't really know him. I never answered the letter and I am sorry about that because he was only young and a little older than I was. He was German and I knew I couldn't be seen going out with a German prisoner of war. I was sorry that I wasn't able to even write back to him.

I never ever felt that I could talk to my mum about anything; she just was not interested in whatever I had to say. On V E Day I had been to the cinema in Scunthorpe with friends. The town was so busy with people laughing, singing, shouting, hugging and generally celebrating and having a lot of fun. There were Americans dancing in the street. I always had to be in by 9.30 pm so I left my friends and started walking home. Along the road there were bushes on either side and I had to walk away from the town to get to my nan's house. As I had almost reached my nan's house I could hear footsteps behind me.

I was outside the back gate near to the back door when the man pushed me hard up against the fence. He was a grown man and I was just a kid. He held me tight against the fencing and I quickly realised that I had to be careful about how I handled this situation. I was very scared but I didn't know what he was going to do. I remember thinking 'Keep calm and talk gently to him, don't let him know you are frightened of him.'

I said to him

'I don't know who you are and I don't know what you are doing this for but my mum and my auntie and gran will be coming along here any minute.'

He stepped back a bit and I managed to loosen his grip and get away from him. It had been snowing and he grabbed hold of me again and got me down flat on my back onto the ground.

He got on top of me and I saw Margaret, who lived next door, saying goodnight to her boyfriend outside the gate. He was on the outside of the gate and she was on the inside. Her family were very strict and their surname was Turpin. Her dad was called Dick Turpin and we used to laugh about that. I instinctively knew that I only had seconds to get away. The man leaned on one arm while he reached down to undo his fly buttons with the other hand. I had seen a similar thing in a film and very quickly realised that this was my only opportunity. I brought my knees up fast and hard into his body and he was yelling out

'You little bitch!'

While this was happening I was calling out to Margaret to help me. She could see what was happening but she just carried on talking to her boyfriend and ignored my pleas. I must have hit him in the right place because he was holding himself and yelling out. That gave me just enough time to get away from him so I jumped up and ran through my gate, into the back door and slammed it shut behind me. I didn't dare put the lock on because I was frightened that my mum or my nan would come home and wouldn't be able to get in so I would be in trouble.

I ran upstairs and peeped out of the heavy lace curtains in the bedroom. I could see the man standing by the back gate. I found out later that he had targeted me and had been watching my movements in and out of the house for several days. He knew who I was but I had no idea that he had followed me home until the attack happened. From the upstairs window I could see him pulling at the back door but it was stuck – I had slammed it behind me so hard because I was so frightened. He probably thought the door was locked. The next thing I could hear was my nan coughing. I was never so relieved to hear that cough!

My mum and nan walked in through the gate and found the man standing by the back door. He said

'Oh good evening Mrs Thomas, Joan has got my bus fare in her pocket.'

My nan said

'Good evening young man.'

Then, to my horror, nan and mum invited him into the house! I was in the bedroom and my nan called out for me to come downstairs. I hesitantly went down and there he was, stood there in the living room smiling. Nan said

'This young man says you have his bus fare in your pocket, you were holding it for him.'

I didn't say anything but went to my coat which by then was hanging in the hallway and I felt in the pocket. There was his money! He must have planted it in my pocket when he held me at the fence. He had slipped the money in there as an alibi in case he was caught.

Nan handed over the money to him and thanked him as she ushered him to the door. Off he went and nan and mum thought what a nice young man he was. They probably thought that I had been out with him. Another time though I could have brought a lad of my own age home and they would have called me the biggest slut going! I was never allowed girl or boy friends into the house. Yet here was a grown, predatory man being invited in!

I started to tell nan and mum what had really happened when nan suddenly put her finger to her mouth and said Sshhh! She walked over to the window and pulled the curtain away. There was the man outside of the window listening to what I was saying. I had never seen my nan and mum move so fast in all my life. They ran a long way to try and catch him but he got away.

The attack was reported to the police and we found out that he had been doing the same thing to other women in the area and had raped a couple of them. He was in the Royal Navy. Mum did say that if I saw him again any time we were out I was to alert her. I could never forgive our neighbour, Margaret, though for not helping me, she *must* have heard me calling out to her.

During the war years mum got married twice more. Her first marriage was in 1939 to a man called Sydney Day who turned out to be a bigamist. The marriage only lasted a few months until mum found out that they weren't legally married! Sydney Day was sent to prison for nine months for bigamy and the scandal and court case made the local newspaper. Mum met and married another man, Sidney Smith, in 1941. They were together for several years until he died.

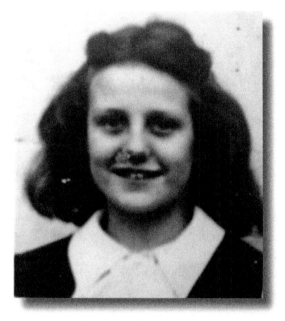

Joan aged 13 years.

4

Rape

In my early teens I was still living in Scunthorpe. We were living in my grandparents' house which was in Diana Street and in a better class of area because my nan and granddad had money. Granddad Charlie was a well-respected civil engineer with his own gang of workmen. He organised the building of roads around Lincoln to link up several of the villages and towns so that traffic could move around more easily. He was in charge and sometimes he drove a steam roller on the roads. He worked hard and earned good money. At the completion of each building project an important local person would cut a ribbon to celebrate the opening of the road network.

Nan and granddad had two pianos and there was always music in their house. I have a few fond memories of that time of all my family playing music and singing together. My granddad played the euphonium and was in the Salvation Army band – and him a staunch conservative as well! Everybody knew and loved Charlie Tuck. He originally came from Norfolk. He was a really kind man and I loved him but I just tolerated my nan. She never gave me any affection and was quite strict. No one in my family put their arms around me, cuddled me or consoled me, ever.

One day I had been out with my friends into town. When we arrived back we sometimes sat in the Jug and Bottle. This was a room in our nearby pub where they sold alcohol and soft drinks, like an off-licence within the pub. We were allowed in there. We always used to giggle our heads off with the lads who lived in the area as well. There was no hanky panky or anything like that; we were all just good friends and had fun together.

I was a well-developed kid at that age and people sometimes said that I looked like a little film star. I was with a group of girls and boys and we were all talking and laughing. I always had to be home by 9 o'clock so I said

'I will have to go home now or else I will be in trouble if I am late.'

One of the boys, a good looking fella, who I thought was about 19, offered to walk me home. I told him it was a long walk and that I had to pass a large old derelict house that frightened me.

He was very polite and said

'I will walk you home if you are frightened.'

He was curious and said he wouldn't mind having a look at the old house. As I had a boy with me I felt safe and so I walked home with him and we were chatting most of the way. We got to a place with fields on one side and the huge 12-bedroomed derelict house on the other side. I was petrified of walking past the house on my own. It looked dark and spooky and it had three gates, one on each side of the large gate with the driveway in the middle. During the war the army requisitioned the house and used it as a headquarters but by that time it was standing empty. Walking past the gates of the large house I often thought that anybody could be hiding in there and could just jump out at me. The road which ran along the back of the house was just as bad because it was lined with hedgerows so I walked past the front of the house as there was always one street light on at the end so at least there was some illumination. My nan's house was not far from there and on the way I had to walk down a little alleyway.

The boy and I walked and chatted and when we got to the big house we were still just talking. I had never walked into the big drive-way before. Suddenly the boy picked me up and pushed me hard up against the gate wall! My legs were dangling above the ground and his broad shoulders were suffocating me; he was so strong that I was choking.

It all happened so quickly, he pushed me so hard that my head was up above his and I was pinned to the wall by his shoulders. He undid his trouser buttons and the ordeal went on so long that I really felt as though he was going to rip me apart. I couldn't breathe. I couldn't scream because his shoulders and chest were suffocating me. I was completely shocked and didn't know what was happening.

I was a virgin and hadn't been with a man, so I didn't really understand what was going on. We were never taught the facts of life in those days. It was so painful and was such an awful violation. I was terrified and thought he would kill me, that I was going to die. I had been raped! I was just 13 years old and would be 14 in a few weeks' time!

Afterwards I dropped to the floor sobbing uncontrollably. I was mortified and in a state of complete shock and numbness. I could feel something warm running down my legs. He handed me his handkerchief to clean the blood off me. I was still sobbing. He didn't say anything to me, nothing at all. He just gave me his handkerchief and walked away.

A woman's virginity is sacred to her and I had suffered an absolutely brutal violation of mine; it was snatched away from me. I just didn't know what to do next! Any man would be locked up for that nowadays. I never saw the boy ever again.

It was a terrible time for me because I never, ever told anybody what had happened and I knew there would be no one indoors when I got home. There would be nobody who would listen because they never wanted to know about me or my problems. This horrendous thing had just happened to me and I thought to myself 'What is the point in going home and telling anyone what has happened, that I had been attacked and raped?' I felt ashamed and that it was all my fault because I had let him walk home with me. I thought 'Well, you have asked for it Joan.'

I was sobbing all the way home and there was nobody in the house when I arrived. I washed my face so no one would see that I had been crying. I sat in the armchair stunned and tried to make sense of what had just happened to me. I just couldn't take it in.

My brother Peter was mostly always nasty to me; it was very rare that he was ever nice to me. Because mum didn't like me, he didn't like me either. He once put a red-hot poker into my back – but more about that later. A while later, when Peter came in, he was drunk. He sat opposite me and could obviously tell by my face that something had happened. He said 'What's the matter with you?' in a condescending sneering manner which made me feel worthless. He was a horrible brother at times. As he was drunk, I didn't say a word in reply. I went to bed in pain, alone and crying.

For many years I told no one about the rape. I had been too trusting and naïve and I blamed myself completely. Even later in my life when the police questioned me in court I never said a word about the rape. The police could have arrested my attacker but I kept it all to myself. I didn't tell anyone or report it or anything. I carried it around with me for years. My violent rape didn't come out until many years later.

Months later I had been out to see some friends and when I arrived back home Peter was there waiting for me. Peter said

'Here you are sis.'

He handed me a half crown, which was quite a lot of money then, and he said

'Treat yourself to the pictures (cinema) and buy yourself some sweets. Spend it all, I don't want any of it back.'

I was so shocked that my brother had been nice to me for once and had treated me to the pictures! It was so rare that I couldn't quite believe it.

After I came back from the cinema I didn't see Peter for several days. After a week I asked my mum and nan where Peter was because I hadn't seen him for a while. They told me he was not coming back and that he had gone away. They wouldn't say any more about it. As far as they were concerned the subject was closed.

I thought it was awful of them not to tell me why Peter had gone away or where he had gone to. Much later I found out that he had joined the army. There was nothing wrong with him joining the army so why couldn't my family tell me? Peter just disappeared from my life with no prior warning, just as my dad had done.

Peter had enlisted with the Grenadier Guards. He joined as a boy recruit and then moved on into the army as a man. He travelled all over the world with the army and I thought how lucky he was because I was the one stuck at home and he was writing to mum about all the exotic places he had visited. I always seemed to get the brunt end of everything, but it was meant to be. In a way I am delighted and I am working it off. I take on whatever comes my way; I take it in my stride and get on with it – I have had to!

5

Work begins

Just before my 14th birthday I left school and I had to find a job. Jobs were fairly hard to come by at that time. The woman in the Labour Exchange told me that there were only domestic jobs available. I didn't mind that and I found a job where I would be working for a lady as a nanny and also carrying out some domestic work. The pay was 15 shillings (75p) a week and that was good because I could give most of that to my mum because she didn't have a husband's wage coming in. I accepted the job and started work a few days later.

I cannot remember my employer's name but I will call her Mrs Smith. When I arrived for work Mrs Smith told me that she would have to go into hospital at some time and wanted me to help with the housework and look after her five children. Also living in the house were her husband and a lodger.

She said

'When I go into hospital you will have to look after the house and get the children up and ready for school. However, it is possible that I may *not* have to go into hospital so then I won't need you any more as I will not be able to afford to keep you on permanently. So the job is only temporary.'

I accepted what she told me and thought no more about it.

It was hard work, I had to get up very early in the morning, get the children ready for school and prepare breakfast so I always felt tired. One day Mrs Smith said to me

'Do you think your mother will let you live-in?'

I said that I would ask my mum when I went home from work

that evening. Mrs Smith said that if she had to go into hospital I would be needed there so I thought it was a good enough reason for me to live-in. When I arrived home I asked mum and she asked me if I was alright there. I said I was. I would never have told her if I wasn't alright, I had learnt to keep my mouth shut and keep my problems to myself. After all, I had been doing that all of my life.

I carried on with the job and I was cleaning and doing everything I was asked to do. In the evenings, around six o'clock, it would seem that everybody in the house vanished and I couldn't understand where they had gone. Mrs Smith told me to sit down and said she was just going along the road for a few minutes and that the children were playing nicely in the other room.

I sat there for a few minutes and then a man walked in; I had never met him in my life before. He sat at the table, took out a cigarette and started talking to me. There was something that I instinctively didn't like about the situation; I felt very uncomfortable. He asked me if I would like a cigarette. I said 'No thank you.' I would not give him eye contact at all and so I kept staring at the fire. He carried on trying to talk to me and I just thought 'Where has everybody gone? Why isn't anyone coming in?' Apparently, as I found out, Mrs Smith had warned other people not to go into that room.

After some time Mrs Smith came back into the room and said to the man

'How did you get on Ernie, any good?'

'No, you can't even melt her,' he replied.

'Oh she's like a lump of ice is she? Well, we will have to see about that, won't we?'

The same thing happened on a few more occasions and each time a different man walked in. No one tried to force themselves on me but they were trying to win me round all of the time. It felt very uncomfortable. One tea-time Mrs Smith said to me

'Look Joan, Ernie is coming round and I want you to go on an errand for me. He is waiting outside in the car. He has got to go and pick something up and I want you to help him.'

So I did as I was told to do and we set off in Ernie's little Austin car.

By this time I knew Scunthorpe like the back of my hand. Ernie started driving along country roads and we drove and drove on and on, further out of town. It started to pour with rain and I didn't have a coat with me. Eventually we pulled up in a place surrounded by trees and I thought to myself 'I don't like this. I don't like this at all. There were no houses or shops around us, just trees. I thought we were going to collect something. What was he up to? I was so naïve! I believed what Mrs Smith had told me that we had to collect a parcel. I trusted her and didn't question her motive at all!

The Austin car was only tiny and I moved as far away as I could from him. He said to me

'Would you like to get out of the car and go for a walk?'

'No, I wouldn't, I want to go back!' I replied.

'We will sit and talk then shall we?'

I wouldn't talk to him and wouldn't answer him when he spoke. Then he said

'Wouldn't you like to undo my flies and play with me?'

I was horrified! I said

'*NO, NO*, I want to go home, take me back!'

I was very scared but at the same time a feeling of great anger and defiance came over me. I tried to be stern with him with my voice but I was so polite as well. Modern kids would have screamed their heads off and hit him! It was the way I was brought up; you speak when you are spoken to. Who do you think is interested in you? Get outside and don't listen to grown-ups' conversation – that is what my mother always said to me.

So I never told them anything and I never learnt anything. I was always shut away from everything. Then Ernie said

'I have had loads of girls up here and they have loved it; they have really enjoyed themselves. Wouldn't you like to try it?'

'*NO*, I want to go back, I want to go back *NOW*!' I yelled.

I just kept looking out of the window; I wouldn't even look at him. I was trying to be stern with him but underneath I was petrified. Luckily, for me, he didn't force the issue but he could have done because I was in a very vulnerable position.

Eventually Ernie took me back to Mrs Smith's house and he had a conversation with her. He said

'No, I couldn't get anything out of her.'

I think it was the way I looked. Lots of people told me I was such a good-looking girl. I think in a way, the men didn't like the idea of forcing themselves on me. Also I was a very polite person and I think that is what may have helped me.

I carried on working but I was very wary all the time. About a week later Mrs Smith said to me

'I won't have to go into hospital after all Joan.'

Apparently she had been pregnant and had had a miscarriage. That is probably the reason why she was unsure whether she would have to go into hospital or not. I began to read between the lines by then. She said

'Do you remember the agreement was that if I couldn't afford to keep you I would have to let you go? Well, you can go home now if you want to. I won't need your help any longer.'

I felt so happy and relieved! I thought I would go home because I hated living there with all those creepy men coming and going and offering me cigarettes and money in exchange for other things! I wanted to get out of there as soon as I could and this was a good excuse for me. I said to her

'Would you write me a reference please because that will help me to get another job after this one has finished?'

'Oh yes, certainly, we will write you a nice reference.'

Then, that morning, she said to me, before her husband had got around to writing the reference,

'We have been talking and the lodger said he would pay your wages for you if you stay here.'

I thought 'Really? Well, I know now why he was offering to do that for me; what did I have to do in return, end up in his bed?' I said

'No, I don't want that thank you; I want to go home if you don't mind.'

I asked if I could just have the reference please. Well, I got the reference and at the bottom they had written "Left of her own accord." That sentence was the worst undoing for me but I didn't know that until sometime later. Today I cannot remember her name, even though I have tried and tried. I suppose I have blocked it out of my memory because it was such a dreadful experience. It was the only way I could deal with it.

After I left that house I had to walk the streets until nearly 12 o'clock at night, waiting for my mum to arrive home from work. No one else was in and I wasn't allowed a front door key. Luckily I happened to be in the right area at the right time when my mum came walking along the street.

'Hello mum,' I said. She said

'What are you doing here?'

'Well, I have got an excellent reference so I will be able to get another job but the lady doesn't want me anymore because she is not going into hospital after all.'

I said that because I thought that if I didn't say I could get another job she would not want me back home. That was alright with her because when she had been drinking she was nice to me. That was the only time she was ever nice to me. So, we went indoors and I made us a cup of tea. I went to bed because I was very tired; I had been up since six o'clock that morning. I slept well right through that night.

The next morning when I woke up I thought I could hear someone crying. It was mum crying and I thought to myself 'I bet auntie Sylvie has been getting on at my mum again.' Auntie Sylvie was a spitfire and she would pick a knife up as quickly as look at you. She was very hot tempered at times and was very fiery in her younger years. Nobody could stop her; she had such a bad temper.

My mother never ever came to see anything I was in at school or to see my work, like most mums do, but the next morning she went out of her way and got up early to go and see Mrs Smith – the woman who had been grooming and procuring me for men! Mum never got up early because she always worked late in the clubs and slept in each morning. I thought it was very strange she was up and out early that day and it was a fair walk to Mrs Smith's house. Why? What was so important? She always had my money. I got my wages and I always handed over money to her for living there and only kept a few shillings back for myself.

I still don't understand why she went to see Mrs Smith because I received a lovely reference from her. Mum read it and saw the wording at the bottom which said that the lodger had offered to pay my wages and the ending which said 'Left of her own accord.' She went mad over that sentence and accused me of wrong-doing but as usual I never had the chance to explain my side of the situation to her. She wouldn't have wanted to know anyway!

That same morning I had just got up and it was the first lay-in I had had since I had been working for Mrs Smith. I always had to get up early and get the kids off to school. Even at the age of 14 I was responsible for someone else's family as well as the three adults!

I went downstairs and picked up my shoes. I had the same clothes on as I had come home in because I hadn't had time to unpack anything. I was carrying a jacket over my arm and as I opened the door into the living room mum had arrived back home and was sitting there crying. I just thought that mum and auntie Sylvie had had an argument – as they often did. My auntie Sylvie screamed at me

'You dirty little bitch, you dirty little scum you! We have heard all about what you have been getting up to! You have been having it off with men in that house!'

'Pardon me?' I stood there dumb-struck; I just couldn't believe my ears!

I was stunned and I thought 'What have I been getting up to?' You see I always had that guilty conscience that I had done something wrong. Mum looked up and said to me

'I have got this reference here and it says "Left of her own accord." What does that mean? So, I want to know why you left of your own accord.' She was thinking about the money; she had this money from me coming in regularly you see. I didn't understand what they meant so I just stood there, looking at them, trying to take in what they were saying. I was bewildered. I said

'I don't understand. What did Mrs Smith say?'

'She said you had been having it off with all of the men who had gone into the house. You are a little slut, you are a prostitute. *GET OUT OF THIS HOUSE! GET OUT OF THIS HOUSE NOW, THIS MINUTE!*

I had both my mother and my aunt screaming at me

'Get out of this house and don't ever come back!'

They didn't give me a chance to say anything more; they just went on and on, screaming at me. Mrs Smith had told mum that I was the one bringing in the men and prostituting in her house! Of course she said that to save her own neck. It was a huge shock to me that mum believed what that woman told her! If she had just said to me

'Joan, tell me what *really* happened.'

I could have told her about the man taking me out in his van miles from anywhere and how scared I was. Also about the other two men she fetched in as well. All of that was a big calamity in my life because I was an honest kid and I couldn't understand it. I didn't know what prostitution was or what the word even meant! How would I ever learn about it? No one told me anything about life.

I always had to do as I was told, so I left the house straight away. I was never going to go back home – that is until I was picked up by the police.

I had been thrown out of my home. I felt absolutely stunned as I left the house and with only £3 in my pocket. I had just got paid and had given the rest of my wages to my mum. I had worked and saved some money but I thought what can I do with £3? Where am I going to go? I walked out of the house and was heartbroken that my own family could have believed such things of me. I wasn't even given an opportunity to defend myself. I felt broken. I have always brought my children up to speak up, to tell their side of things, to say what is on their minds. I gave my children the chance to speak up; what I suffered as a child was never going to happen to them!

I walked the streets for a while bewildered and wondering what I could do. I had some good friends and I bumped into Maisie Booth and her sister, with their untidy peroxide hair and really thick red lips. I liked them but my nan would never have let me associate with them; they wouldn't have been good enough for her. I was never allowed to invite a friend into my nan's house, not one friend. I was normally such a happy-go-lucky person but I felt utterly dejected and alone walking those streets.

Maisie could see my tears and distress and she said

'What's the matter Joan? What's up with you?'

'My mum and auntie have thrown me out of my house and I have nowhere to go. I don't know what to do,' I said

'Come home with us; there is only granddad at home.'

Their granddad was looking after them. I asked if their granddad would mind me going home with them. They said

'Of course it will be alright, he won't mind. In fact, you can sleep with us.'

I was so grateful to them, I couldn't thank them enough.

They didn't have much money and were so scruffy. Nan was always telling me at home to go and wash my hands or my hair so I always looked spick and span. I stayed there for two days and nights and I am not joking when I say I was bitten to death by fleas! The house was riddled with them. I could feel them jumping all over me. What was I to do? I either had to walk the streets or scratch myself to death? I was frightened to move because there were three of us in the bed.

All I had was the £3 I had left home with. I could not take food from them without giving them something and contributing, so I gave their granddad £2 and that left me with £1 in my pocket. I couldn't bear to stay there any longer and I told them I would have to go home. They said

'Stay here, you are alright here, don't go home.'

I couldn't stay there another night with them; the house was riddled! That wasn't their fault either, they were only young. Bless them; I will never forget them and their kindness. It touches me even now thinking about them.

I walked the streets all the next day. I walked to the very end of the High Street because I knew there was a café there. When I arrived outside the café I saw a sign on the window advertising "help wanted" so I went in and was given an interview. The woman asked me if I had left school and I had because I was 14. They were looking for someone to do the washing up and clear the tables in the café and change the beds in the bed and breakfast part of the café. The wages were 15 shillings a week, plus all my food was provided and I would get a bed. I was so pleased to be offered the job.

Unfortunately I couldn't start the job until two days' time so I walked the streets again until it got dark. I walked to the big old house and went to the side door which had once been the staff entrance. The house was huge, dirty and empty. I was feeling so low and worthless then that I didn't care what happened to me anymore. Awful flashbacks of the rape came flooding back to me but, as frightened as I was, it was getting dark and I had to find refuge for the night. The house was the only shelter I could find. I had nowhere else to go. If I had walked the streets all night I could have ended up with my throat cut. My house wasn't very far away but I just couldn't go back there. They had thrown me out and I couldn't go through all that again; they were probably still very angry and would just scream at me to leave a second time.

At the big house I found myself in the forecourt; some of the glass was missing in the front door. Luckily there was a bright moon that night so visibility was good. I went inside. I had my coat on and I used my handbag as a pillow and I laid down on the floor. There were bits of broken brick, glass and grit everywhere; half the floor was missing. It was cold and eerie as I laid there and I didn't get one wink of sleep. I just stared at the moon and as time went on I watched it move across the window and around the house.

Eventually I started hearing the noise of cars and I guessed it must be about 6 o'clock in the morning. I thought I would walk into town and use the ladies toilet to dust myself down, wash my hands and face, comb my hair and tidy myself up – I must have looked dusty from sleeping rough. I was trying to feel positive and was pleased with myself because I had a new job to go to. At least I would have a roof over my head and food to eat.

I had been away from home for a few days by then and I was walking along the road when a policeman came face-to-face with me. He was a short man and he was wearing a very long overcoat. He said

'Hello and where have you been?'

I explained that I had been to a friend's house because she had had a birthday party and I had stayed the night there and was now on my way home. He asked my address and told me to go on home and said goodbye to me. I went on my way but he knew that Diana Street, the road my nan's house was in, was in a different direction. He followed me and then he cut through a side road. He came face-to-face with me once again and that was it! I thought 'Oh, I really am in trouble now. What have I done this time?' He said

'You are coming with me.'

He stopped at a policeman's hut which looked just like the Tardis featured in the Doctor Who television programme years later. He unlocked it and said sternly

'You had better tell me your right name and give me the correct address where you live this time – where your mother lives.'

I told him my address and he said that I would be in trouble if I had lied. I pleaded with him that I had told him the truth.

He told me that my family had reported me missing. I had my mum, my auntie Sylvie and my nan and granddad in the house and they thought they should do something because they had expected me back home after the row. But I had done as I was told! They threw me out and I was never to go back and darken their door again. They had screamed it so loudly that I didn't want to go back.

That episode really killed any love I had for them.

Fate had dealt me the rough end once again. I had found myself a good job to go to in the café. I would be living in, so I would have a roof over my head in a respectable place, I would get all my food and a wage packet, clearing tables, washing up, making beds and serving food. I thought life would be good with this job. I would be so good and work hard and work my way up in the business – I was always ambitious as well. If that policeman hadn't seen me going around that corner, he wouldn't have known I wasn't going home and things would have been so different. But it was meant to be I suppose.

The policeman took me back to my nan's house and knocked on the front door. My mum was curling her hair and getting ready for work. By then she was a head chef in a big canteen in the Appleby & Frodingham steelworks. She also worked in the evenings playing the piano. She had to go out and find work because she had lost her widow's pension by marrying a second time. She just looked down at me and said

'Oh, we have got you back again have we? You have decided to come home have you? Do you know that I have reported you missing to the police?'

She didn't say anything nice like 'Oh, thank goodness you are safe.' She showed no emotion whatsoever, just scorn.

After the policeman left, mum finished getting ready for work. I remember thinking that it was such a bind for her, having me back. She said

'Well, you can clean the bedroom out and make yourself look tidy as well.'

I felt like a dreadful fugitive and thought that nobody in that house loved me; that they all hated me. They must have told my granddad what they had accused me of doing and I thought he must hate me, so I had no love or friendship coming from my granddad then, although I still loved him. My nan must have believed it as well because neither of them spoke to me.

My auntie Sylvie was there and she was bossing me around as she

always did. I worked in my room until dinner tin.
out and shook them and polished everything I could ᵥ
time auntie Sylvie shouted up to the window

'Joan, come on downstairs, there's fish and chips here for you.

I could have screamed my head off because I was so hungry but I didn't dare run down or look too excited about it. I was obedient and said

'Yes, alright then.'

I went downstairs and had the fish and chips and a cup of cocoa. It felt wonderful to have a decent meal; I hadn't eaten for such a long time. I ate the fish and chips and I then went and sat upstairs out of the way of everyone.

Life went on like that for a few more days and then mum told me that the police were coming to interview me. I immediately thought 'What have I done now?' It was the same scenario again and I thought of what I could possibly have done to get the police involved. Did I tell a lie, is that what they were coming for? A week earlier, when the policeman had stopped me, I had lied about where I had been but we had got over that one. I was able to think quickly for myself, I had to.

It was early teatime when a policeman and policewoman came to see me to ask questions. They started asking me questions about mine and Peter's childhood. I thought to myself 'If I told you the truth you would never believe me.' Then the questions moved on to my stay and work at Mrs Smith's house. The policeman said

'What pub did you meet the men in Joan?'

'The Bluebell,' I replied.

I told them that because it was a lively and notorious pub in the area and lots of Irish men went in there. It was loud and noisy and often glasses were thrown across the pub and there was fighting inside and outside. Hundreds of Irish people came over from Ireland to work in the steelworks. It was just like one of Catherine Cookson's stories. A lot of the men were young and they could earn regular wages in the steelworks whereas back in Ireland jobs were scarce.

policeman said

'Where did you go with the men you met in the pub Joan? Did you go for a walk with them?'

I replied

'Oh, we went to all sorts of places, doorways and down Winter Road.' Winter Road was a very long road which went down to Normandy, a big estate not far from my nan's house. It was the only road I could think of.

Then he asked

'What did you do with those men Joan?'

'Oh, the men used to make love to me,' I replied.

'Were they intimate with you?'

'Yes, of course they were.'

'What other men did you go out with Joan?'

'I went out with hundreds of Irishmen.' I was really daring and I had never been like that in my life. Where did it all come from? Why did I tell so many lies? I felt so bitterly angry and I just wanted to get my own back on my family in some way.

Of course, I didn't do myself any good at all telling all those lies. They were all lies! It was very quiet in the house and all the family were listening. You could hear a pin drop.

The questions went on

'So, how often did you do it?'

'Oh, lots of times, I went with lots of men.'

I think they twigged that I was lying and I carried on and on because my mum and auntie Sylvie had believed all the lies from everyone else and so I thought I if they wanted to hear lies I would give them lies! I was so furious and bitter and I did it to hurt my mum.

I thought to myself 'You want to know, I will tell you what I think you want to hear.'

In reality I hadn't done any of those things. I was working long hours and living in, when did they think I had the time to do all that? I thought they would realise I was telling lies because what I was telling them was so far-fetched.

I didn't do myself any good at all but I felt so let down and betrayed by my mum. It was one of the blackest days of my life when I think that it was my mum and my auntie who threw me out – I was just a kid! They believed this stranger, this evil woman who was fetching men into her house and grooming and procuring young girls for them! It had happened to other girls before me.

The policeman and policewoman had hardly spoken to the rest of my family in the house. Then I thought oh, I have got myself into a lot of trouble now, telling all those lies, but I felt very let down by their lack of support for me. I loved my granddad and I didn't want him to think badly of me. I wanted him to say 'You are a good girl, you are not like that, and I don't believe a word of it.' But not one of them defended me or took my side and that is what I hated about my family.

The police told me that Mrs Smith was trying to encourage me into prostitution and that I was never to go back to Scunthorpe again, ever! You see this is how it affected my life; I was ruined by it. Not once did mum ask me what really happened. My mum and auntie are in spirit now and of course they know the truth but it has been very hard for me to learn to forgive them. For years and years I only ever wanted to please my mum. I loved her and found it very hard to turn my back on her. The policeman wrote it all down. I never mentioned the rape; I never spoke about it to anyone. I was in enough trouble!

After the police interview there was a full investigation. They went right back to when Peter and I had lived in Ravendale Street, right back to when my dad had committed suicide. They wanted to know who looked after us after my father died, when there was no man in the house. They knew that my mother played the piano in the working men's clubs and pubs and they asked who was looking after us while she was at work.

The police also investigated Mrs Smith as well; her house and the men she had tried to procure me for. She had obviously been in trouble before and the police knew all about her. I wasn't the first girl she had employed. The police realised then that I was innocent.

The policeman asked me what I wanted to do when I grew up. I said I wanted to be an artist and I was determined that I was going to be a famous artist. He said

'Really? So you think you can draw do you?'

'As a matter of fact I can. Well, you asked me didn't you?' I said indignantly.

I got really huffy over that because that was another thing that I was speaking the truth about. I felt they were trampling all over me and trying to rub me out as if I wasn't there and didn't exist. No one looked up and said 'Oh yes, she is very good at drawing.' I could produce full blown portraits at eight years old! People said to me 'Who is that you have drawn?' when they came in with my mum from the club and they had been drinking. I used to shrug my shoulders and say 'I dunno, it's just a face.' Men and women, dogs and cats, anything I wanted to draw I did it and it was just there. I put my pencil to the paper and I just drew.

The policeman said

'Alright then, if you can draw, do some drawings and we will come back in a couple of days' time and have a look at them.'

So I got the newspaper out because I had to protect the polished-top table and couldn't bear to damage the tablecloth by drawing on it! I got my large-size paper out and produced some portraits. I copied a few from the newspaper adverts. For two days I sat there drawing. I drew portraits of a man and a woman together, head and shoulders. I drew a woman with a glamorous hairstyle. I loved glamour. I made clothes like the film stars wore. I knitted every one of Lana Turner's jumpers; I had every one of them.

A couple of days later the policeman and policewoman came back, saw the drawings and said

'Oh, we didn't know you could draw like that.'

'Well, you did ask me to draw and I have.' I replied. The result of that went in my favour later as time went on.

The full police investigation was written out and a final report was produced for the court. It took a long time and I had to live through all of that. I didn't hear any more from the police for a long time – until I was summoned to appear in court.

6

Jobs and justice

I carried on living at home with my family until I found myself another good job. I had a good character but nothing followed me around like bad issues. I got a job with four Irish doctors and I was to live-in. It got me out of my own home and I longed for that. I didn't want to live with my family any longer; there was an awful feeling and atmosphere there.

The people who ran the doctors' house, the caretaker and his wife, answered the phone and cleaned out the surgeries. I was to help them and learn the different aspects of the job. The Irish doctors were very kind and friendly. I loved the Irish and Scunthorpe was full of Irish people at that time. When the Second World War came many Irish people worked in the steel works making guns and ammunition. My mum's sister, auntie Violet, also worked in the steelworks. She drove a crane, like those big ones in the dockyards, and yet she was a lah-di-dah sort of lady and wore the most beautiful clothes.

I started my new job. The doctors' surgery was in a lovely big four-bedroom, double bay-fronted house in the High Street. I loved living there and felt proud to be seen coming out of such a lovely house. My bedroom wasn't very nice but it was quite enough for me. I had a chest of drawers where I kept my drawing things in the bottom drawer with my pencils and paints. I didn't care about clothes as long as I had my drawing equipment.

The caretaker's wife did a lot of baking and she asked me what my favourite food was. I said I loved custard pies when they were baked in the oven. She used to bake those for me – but her husband seemed a bit dodgy. He said

'Ooh we have got a lovely young woman living with us.'

I quickly picked up on the sneaky way he had about him. I hadn't put a foot wrong but I knew that everywhere I went my good looks followed me. My mum and dad were both good-looking. I was really very happy living and working there but unfortunately it was to be short-lived.

I helped to clean the surgeries and upstairs where they all did their recreation. In the evenings the doctors wrote out their notes. I was taught to operate the switchboard and I answered phone calls. I had never used a telephone before and sometimes I found it difficult to understand what people were saying and so it took some time to get used to. One time I was told off by one of the doctors because I couldn't understand a patient. The patient put the receiver down on me and I hadn't taken a phone number so that the doctor could ring him back. The doctor found out who the patient was eventually and dealt with it – the patient must have rung back.

Opposite our house In the High Street was a photographer's shop where photos were taken and artwork and paintings were displayed in the windows. I thought that with my first wages I would buy something from there. So I saved up a couple of weeks' wages and off to the shop I went. As I walked towards the photographer's shop I saw my auntie Sylvie. She shouted out

'Have you heard? Your mother has been taken to court.'

I was shocked! She said

'Yes, and you have got to go to court as well, the police are after you. You have got to go to court next Tuesday.'

The day had started off sunny, I had a job, money in my pocket and the shop on the other side of the road was an art and photography shop – what could be better? That is when the bomb was dropped and my experience with the police and court system began.

⚬

Later that day a policeman arrived at the doctors' surgery with a summons for me and insisted that my employer make sure I appeared in court in a few days' time. I was so upset that I threw myself on the bed crying.

'That's it; they won't want me working here now because I am in trouble with the police.'

I really thought I would lose my job. One of the lady doctors gave me a hug and said

'You are a good girl, you are lovely and we are going to write a good letter to the court speaking up for you and saying that while you have lived with us you have worked hard and not done a thing wrong.'

She told me that my job would still be there when I got back from court. I was so relieved to hear that!

The next evening there was a knock at the front door. I went to open it and it was my mother! She said

'I have just come to ask, are you pregnant?'

I was very indignant and said

'No, I am not!'

'Oh good' she said and off she went. That was all she had to say to me! I was horrified that she could think such a thing of me and I didn't like her for that. I didn't see her again until the day we met in court.

The morning I was due in court I felt quite relaxed about it. I wasn't afraid and I was certain that I would be going back to my job and new home after the hearing, especially as my employers were going to speak up for me. I said

'Cheerio, I will empty the bucket when I get back.'

They told me to borrow the bike so that I could cycle to the court, which was at the bottom of the High Street. So off I cycled to court. I was still in my working clothes because I had no idea I would not be going back there ever again. When I arrived at court I didn't have to wait and I went straight in – escorted by police. There wasn't two pennyworth of me, what could I have done to escape from the police?

I was taken into a very old courtroom with a colourful stained-glass window near the ceiling. In front of me was a bench with four people sitting behind it. They asked my name and address. There were two policemen standing guard, one at each door. My mum was sitting about six feet away from me and was wearing a turban on her head. We were not allowed to speak to each other and I had no idea what was going on or what I was there for. The four people sitting at the bench started reading out a list of evidence and discussing why I was there and then papers were passed around. They asked me what I wanted to do. They said to me

'We believe that you are quite an accomplished little artist.'

I replied that I was and that I wanted to be a professional artist. One of the policemen walked over with my suitcase and got out all my pictures which were also passed around. I thought 'That's mine and that one is mine, so is that one'. They had no right to take all my drawings, they were my personal property. I never got them back. I never saw them again and there was a lot of work in that case.

Then the evidence was read out regarding Mrs Smith and how she had tried to procure me for men and encourage me into prostitution. This is where my mum got to learn the truth about me but it was too late, the damage had been done. I was for it and I think that was why she had tears in her eyes because she was hearing the truth. She was sorry and knew she couldn't do anything to change the situation.

The court people said that Peter and I had been neglected since we were small children. We had been left on our own so many times, even through the war years with all the bombing and destruction. It was a clear case of neglect. The police had also questioned the neighbours and were told that there was never anybody there. Sometimes they could hear parties at night-time. Some nights mum brought people home from the club and the music and partying carried on at home.

The court case continued and I just sat there. I turned around to look at my mum and I could see tears in her eyes. I thought 'What have I done to my mum? I must have done something awful, look at her.' I felt so sorry. I wanted to cry myself but I thought 'No, I have got to be brave, I must not cry.' I looked up at the stained-glass window. The four complete strangers were busy conferring amongst themselves in hushed voices and I heard them say '18 years'.

What did I do wrong?

I started crying when they said '18 years' and I thought 'Oh that's it now, I am not going to see anybody for 18 years.' I thought I was going to prison. A policewoman came and put her arms around me and told me not to cry. A policeman was standing behind me as well and I thought 'Why have I got the police with me?' I just didn't understand that part of it. I turned around and looked at mum. She was standing there all alone with tears in her eyes. I thought 'I am so sorry mum, I didn't mean to hurt you.' I lived with that guilt for years after that.

After more discussion one of the people on the bench said

'Right Joan, you are not allowed to go home. We do not want you to associate with your mother ever again.'

The police wouldn't let me speak to mum or even say goodbye. The policewoman still had her arms around me, I was crying and saying

'I have hurt my mum, I have hurt my mum.'

She said

'Your mother doesn't love you; that is why we are here in court today. She has done some awful things and has left you on your own for most of your life.'

'No, you don't know what you are saying; she's not like that, I love my mum.'

It took years, until I was well into my teens, to admit to myself that my mum didn't love me.

I was made a ward of court. I was escorted into a police car and driven all the way to Lincoln. I was sent to a remand home! There were no foster homes in the area at that time and I had to be taken away from my mum. I was only 14 years old! I was driven away and I wasn't told whereabouts the home was. I was to live in a remand home with girls who had broken the law and committed crimes.

7

Leaving home for good

I promised myself that I would never go back home again because there was no one I wanted to see. My family didn't love me. There wasn't a children's home near where I lived and I was not allowed to associate with my mother so I was sent to a remand home which was in Lincoln, a two-hour drive away.

The police drove me to a big imposing house and I was handed over. It was a church home called Steep Hill House Voluntary Remand and Training Home for Girls. The two women who ran the home just ordered me about and told me what to do. I wasn't asked questions or allowed the chance to say anything. I didn't matter. When I was growing up adults frequently used the saying 'Children should be seen and not heard.'

My clothes were taken from me and burnt. I was shown to a small bedroom and told that I would be staying there but I was not to sit on the bed. I could only sit when I was told to. I had to have a bath but I had nothing with me, no wash-bag or clean clothes. I had arrived straight from court. I didn't even have my drawings or pencils with me; they were the best possessions I had ever had. I am not sure if the two women in charge were nuns or not but we called them sisters. The two sisters were looking for clothes to fit me. Some of the clothes they found were awful and I thought 'No, not that!' They made me put on a dress which was much too small for me. It was too tight and it flattened my chest. I wasn't allowed to speak or choose something myself, my opinion didn't matter. They eventually found a dress and said 'That will do.'

That was a dark and depressing time in my life because I was put into a remand home and was treated very sternly. There wasn't room to segregate me from the criminals so I just had to get on with it. Talk about a church home! We had grey uniforms with royal blue piping on the coats and hats. I was not allowed into the main house for some time. I was kept like a fugitive in the annexe situated at one end of the home.

There was a long pathway linking the main house to the annexe and that is where I stayed at first. I thought I had done something so bad and so I stopped talking completely. No one wanted to hear what I had to say so what was the point of talking? I wasn't charged with any crime as the other girls had been; I was put there because there was nowhere else for me to go. I felt utterly dejected and alone. Everything had been taken away from me. Why was this happening to me?

I sat in a chair and looked up at the wall. I saw a framed poem by Rudyard Kipling entitled *If.*

IF

If you can keep your head when all about you
Are losing theirs and blaming it on you,
If you can trust yourself when all men doubt you,
But make allowance for their doubting too;
If you can wait and not be tired by waiting,
Or being lied about, don't deal in lies,
Or being hated, don't give way to hating,
And yet don't look too good, nor talk too wise:

If you can dream – and not make dreams your master;
If you can think – and not make thoughts your aim;
If you can meet with Triumph and Disaster
And treat those two impostors just the same;
If you can bear to hear the truth you've spoken
Twisted by knaves to make a trap for fools,
Or watch the things you gave your life to, broken,
And stoop and build 'em up with worn-out tools:
If you can make one heap of all your winnings

And risk it on one turn of pitch-and-toss,
And lose, and start again at your beginnings
And never breathe a word about your loss;
If you can force your heart and nerve and sinew
To serve your turn long after they are gone,
And so hold on when there is nothing in you
Except the Will which says to them: 'Hold on!'
If you can talk with crowds and keep your virtue,
Or walk with Kings – nor lose the common touch,
if neither foes nor loving friends can hurt you,
If all men count with you, but none too much;
If you can fill the unforgiving minute
With sixty seconds' worth of distance run,
Yours is the Earth and everything that's in it,
And – which is more – you'll be a Man, my son!

The poem was very apt but I felt too numb and dumb at the time to understand it. I appreciate the poem now and can see how appropriate it was at that time.

Some days later I was taken to another building across a long yard. We went into a small room full of books and I had to stay there until I was told otherwise. I was to get up in the morning, wash myself, get dressed and stay in the room. My meals were brought in to me. Someone knocked the door and told me my food was outside the door on a tray. I had to wait a few minutes for the person to go so that I didn't speak to anyone. I was told when it was time for bed. I had been ostracised and was kept prisoner like that for another week with no one to talk to. I have always been an outgoing and friendly person but at that time I hit rock-bottom, believing that I was very evil and wicked.

One day I heard children laughing and playing and I wondered where the noise was coming from. I tried pressing my face against the window pane. Outside there was a matron I had not seen before. She was throwing a ball up for the girls to catch. She must have seen me because she beckoned for me to join them. I had a sob in my throat; someone had actually realised I was there!

Of course I didn't know how to get outside but I eventually found my way and oh, how wonderful it felt to get out into the fresh air and the sunshine! I slowly began to join in with the games but I felt so alien and detached from it all. It all seemed so unreal to me. No one was talking to me, they were ignoring me. Anyway, things changed after the new matron arrived at the house. Sister Hemming was her name and the other one was Sister Galixey.

❧

After the first two or three weeks in the home I was allowed into the big house. The housekeeper asked me what I would like to do. She took me into the common room; it was recreation time and early evening. It was quite dark in there and I sat on the arm of the settee. I didn't feel like I was included in anything because they had shut me away. So I sat on the arm of the settee until somebody told me where I should sit. The housekeeper said

'What can I get for you Joan? What would you like to do?'

She seemed kind and it felt very nice just being spoken to normally. So I replied

'I would like a piece of paper and a pencil please.'

She gave me the paper and pencil and I drew a little girl who was sitting at the table. Her name was Margaret and she had loose curly hair. She was busy playing with something and I was the only person drawing. None of the girls spoke to me; I still felt like a stranger.

At the end of recreation everything was packed away and the housekeeper said

'Do you mind if I have a look at what you have drawn Joan?'

I gave the drawing to her and she said

'Oh, you have drawn Margaret, that's wonderful.'

She took the drawing with her; she didn't give it back to me but I didn't think any more about it. The housekeeper had been friendly to me and the staff obviously trusted her. So after that I started talking again. At first I just said 'Yes' or 'No'; there was no full conversation.

The housekeeper felt sorry for me because I had been on my own and had not spoken to anyone so she asked if she could take me out. She took me to the local museum, bless her. I wish I could meet her now and say thank you. I would really like to be on a committee and say to all those stuffy, fuddy-duddy people who sit on those committees, 'Have you ever been in a home? You live by their harsh rules. I was humiliated and I was already hurting from the way I had been treated throughout my life. Why would you send anyone there?' No one in the home sat any of the girls down and told them what had gone wrong or how we could change things. Everything was decided for us; we had no say in it at all. There was no talking, counselling or therapy in those days – just punishment.

When we arrived in the main house the matron said I had to go to the hospital to be examined by a doctor and she was going to take me there. I didn't know why I had to go there; no one told me any more than that.

When we arrived at the hospital I was shown into a room with a big bed-like contraption. It looked like you had to put your legs up on it. I was told to strip off my underclothes and get up onto the bed. I had to place my legs on the rings, which meant my legs were wide apart. I was so frightened and I just wanted to run away but I was made to do this awful thing. A stern man in a white coat came into the room. I didn't know who he was or what he was going to do! He inserted a tool of sorts into me. I hated what was being done to me. I wasn't pregnant but supposing I was, it could have been dangerous!

I realise now what they were doing but of course I didn't have a clue then. Did they think I had a disease? What were they looking for? No one spoke at all. While I was being examined the matron stood at the back of the bed and I felt so embarrassed and so humiliated. What was my life doing to me?

The remand home was at 56 Steep Hill, Lincoln, an address that will be imprinted on my mind forever. Lincoln was a beautiful city then with a river running through it. To climb Steep Hill you had to hold onto rails and there was a cathedral right on the top. I was enthralled at how imposing and majestic it looked sitting there proudly overlooking the city.

We had to go to the cathedral every Sunday. I was given the job of scrubbing the flagstone pathway leading to the cathedral. I had a bucket of boiling soapy water, a thick industrial scrubbing brush, which I could barely pick up, and no kneeling mat. If I had dared to ask for a kneeling mat I would have been punished and so I just got on with the scrubbing. One Sunday, while we were getting ready to go to the cathedral, I found I couldn't walk. I looked down and my knee was swollen.

'Get your shoes on Thomas,' ordered the sister, to which I replied 'I am sorry but I can't walk because my knee hurts.'

"Let me have a look at you. Woe betide you if you are trying to get out of going to church, you will be severely punished!'

When sister then looked at my knee she called the doctor in straight away. Again she said

'You will be in trouble if there is nothing wrong with you.'

She didn't want any scandal. The doctor put some brown ointment on my knee, put a crepe bandage around it and told me to sit and rest it. I heard him say

'I do believe that this child has housemaid's knee.'

After that I was put to work in the laundry room.

Work in the laundry meant we had to do the whole week's washing and ironing for the entire house. They had washing machines and I was responsible for washing all the laundry for all of the girls and all the towels. I felt that they really were trying to punish me because others didn't have the same workload to do as I did. Every time I dipped my hands into the water I was shouted at

'Go on, get rubbing and rub hard!'

When tea-time came my fingers had swollen up with big blisters and water oozing out of them. Then my fingers started bleeding and the skin had got really tight. I went to Sister Hemming and asked

'Could I please have something to put on my fingers because they are so painful?'

She shouted out so that everyone could hear

'Oh, did you all hear about poor old Joan, she's got poorly hands. Get to your seat! '

My hands were so painful but I just had to get on with it. I had been brought up with cold water all my life. No wonder I got blisters, I wasn't used to hot water. At home if we wanted hot water to have a bath or good wash after playing or before going to bed we put the kettle on. I had to learn to wash myself and even to this day I wash my hands in cold water.

I lived in the remand home in Lincoln for two periods of six months. I had to go back to court after the first six months so that the authorities could extend my incarceration there.

After one year I was glad to get out of that place. When I left there I got taken back to court again; this was the third time now. I was a year older, I had good references, I had behaved myself and our behaviour was recorded daily. My art work was shown to the court and after some discussion they said

'Well, we have decided to send you to a different home and it is in Leeds.'

I thought that sounded alright; I had never been to Leeds. They told me the house was called Bethany House and it was at a place called Headingley. I was to be sent to Bethany House and I would be able to attend Leeds College of Art. I couldn't wait!

Steep Hill House.

8

Hopes raised and dashed

I was moved to Bethany House in Headingley near Leeds. I had committed no crime and yet I was in another remand home living alongside girls who had broken the law. One girl was a gangster's moll, another was a black marketeer and another had attempted to murder her neighbour with hammer blows to the head because he kept bullying and assaulting her dad. Some of the others were there because they repeatedly broke the law. Many of the girls received presents or parcels from their families. All I got was sixpence a week, which the home gave me. I received no parcels or visits from any of my family.

When I first went to Bethany House I had quite a shock because there was a very long table and everybody had their work to do. The table was set up with a huge teapot placed on top of it. The tea was full of saccharine and it tasted absolutely awful! I asked if I could make myself a small pot of tea without sweeteners. I made my own pot of unsweetened tea and I have never taken sugar in my tea since.

The routine of the house was that there were two girls working in the kitchen as well as the cook. If cook wanted you to prepare vegetables, she told you the amount she wanted cleaning and peeling. The washing-up was done by hand; we didn't have machines then. They baked around 18 loaves of bread at a time which were then stored in a long, tall cupboard in the kitchen.

We only had one slice of bread each per day; we didn't dare ask for more! Can you imagine how hard that bread became? We never had fresh bread until it was all used up. We just had to get used to it or go hungry. We had porridge with salt in it, never sugar. We had one teaspoonful of jam each per day. The meals were boiled potatoes and fish or meat at lunchtime. Some of it was edible and we just had to get used to it.

It wasn't too bad there; I liked the company more than anything else. When I first went there, it was nearly tea-time and the table had been set. I was given a sandwich made of thick bread with one slice of corned beef – and that was it. As an honour on a Sunday the matron came in, pulled up her armchair and sat there with her full-grown Dalmatian dog beside her. She broke up cake with her fingers and fed it to the dog. We all just glared at the dog because we only had cake on Sundays. They certainly didn't believe in spoiling us!

The matron's name was Mrs Dunlop and her husband played the piano for the BBC. One day one of the men working at the home asked what matron's name was. He called her Mrs Welldone and I couldn't stop laughing because she did look well done. She was stern and had deep grooves in her face but she was alright really – most of the time anyway.

We did sewing, which entailed repairing sheets and clothing and anything else that needed mending. We helped in the laundry as well.

To lighten things up in the rigid routine, we often played tricks on the young girls who hadn't been there for very long. We got gloves and put a lipstick in each of the fingers and then we tied two brooms together. We then tied a glove to the brooms and went outside and tapped on the windows. The moon was shining and we killed ourselves with laughter and made so much noise it was a wonder matron didn't catch us. We sneaked food up to the bedrooms at night, sat on top of the beds and had a midnight feast. We pooled all the food together and shared it out.

There was another girl called Joan there, who lived just outside of Scunthorpe and she and I became friends. She was brought up by her dad only. I don't know what she did to be in the same home as me but after she arrived we played the piano together. I sat at one end playing and she sat at the other end. We sang our heads off and everyone else cried with laughter. They said 'Ooh, do that again.' I couldn't play the piano for toffee but I used to act about on it. It was great fun.

My friend, Rosemary, and I were on kitchen duty and we had to prepare lunch every day for a week. We cooked fish, boiled potatoes and peas, followed by sponge pudding and custard. One particular day, dinner was nearly ready and Rosemary's bra strap broke. She was only short but she was rather plumpish. She had big eyes and a real curved-up top lip. I still drank people's faces in. I liked her and we both got on well. Her parents sent her postal orders and parcels and so her life wasn't that bad. They still loved her even though she had been taken away from home. She said

'Oh bugger, my blasted bra strap has broken and we are supposed to be dishing up lunch in a few minutes!'

'I am sure I have got a safety pin behind the lapel on my coat. Come on, I will mend it for you,' I urged.

So, off we went to get the safety pin. We were walking through the hallway and there was a heavy swing door with thick pebble-type glass in it. Rosemary pushed the door quite lightly and as she did this the glass cracked and broke into big jagged slivers which started falling out of the door and tinkling onto the floor. The glass fell her way and as she put her arms up to protect herself I could see the glass slicing into her arms and hands, just like meat being cut off for kebabs. It was just awful! She was a plump girl and she had great big gashes everywhere with bubbles of fat showing underneath. Blood was splashing all over the place.

I have always reacted quickly and so I grabbed hold of her arms and put them behind her and said

'Now, turn round and walk to the office and I will get the first aid box!' I didn't know where the first aid box was but I found it and told her I would put some dressings on her arms for her. I didn't want her to see her arms because they looked dreadful and I didn't want her to pass out. I got a big roll of cotton wool, cut it in half and wrapped half around each arm. She was complaining and crying that her arms were hurting. I called an ambulance and then the matron came in and asked what was going on. I had blood splashed all over me, on my legs and my shoes – and I had to go and serve lunch!

The ambulance arrived to take her to the hospital and Rosemary said

'Can Joan come to the hospital with me please?'

'No, she can't!' said matron – and that was it!

'Please let Joan come with me, she looked after me.'

But I was not allowed to go with her. Where was the comfort for the poor terrified girl?

Later on Rosemary wrote to her mum and dad and told them what I had done for her. I hadn't really done much, I had just been sensible and a good friend. Rosemary's parents lived in Brixton in London and they came to the house on their motorbike and asked if they could take me out. They said

'What would you like to do Joan?'

They had heard that the Dolly Sisters were on at the cinema, with Betty Grable and June Haver. I have still got the film because my grandson sent to America to get me the film as it was a part of my early life.

Oh, the hats and gowns and furs that the girls wore or draped over their arm! I loved it all and the colours were so vibrant and wonderful. I took it all in; the shoes, the clothes, the style, the make-up, everything. I was so in awe of it all. It was right up my street. It was just the best reward they could have given me. They didn't have a lot of money but they took both of us out for a meal of fish and chips afterwards and it was all fantastic. I will never forget that episode and their kindness.

As time went on my behaviour record was excellent and so I became a 'trustee'. Most of the girls had come from broken homes and several of them had tried to run away at different times. They were always eventually caught by the police and returned to the home but it meant another six months was added to their sentence. I was charged with talking to the girls and explaining that if they absconded they would eventually be caught and returned and their stay in the home would be even longer. I had to dissuade them from running away. It worked most of the time as we got to know each other better and became friends.

Leeds had trams then. Wonderful things trams were; they were always regular and on time. I remember one day I was allowed to go into Leeds. I loved Leeds because it was like a small London to me. It was cosmopolitan, and it was *with it*. That's what I was, *with it*. I wanted a buzz around me – I am still like that today – but I had to be back by 9.30 pm so I was never able to see the end of a film.

I was fortunate to be allowed to attend Leeds College of Art and I was very successful for the short time I was there. I tried to get a job in the printing room because I thought I could work my way up in the organisation and eventually become a fashion designer. I thought if I could get into the advertising room then I could learn how to set a page out. I thought I could learn a lot by being in a place like that.

Students were split into different groups to study fashion, commerce and advertising. I was in the fashion group and we were asked to study a top-class piece of furniture. It could be a chaise longue in the foyer of a hotel or something similar. We were given examples of what was required; a lady in full evening dress and high-heeled shoes, her husband could be leaning over talking to her or you could have a waiter coming in with cocktails on a little silver tray. Everything had to be ultra-modern. Well, I hadn't been anywhere. I had only been in the home and looking in magazines and that was about the limit of my experience!

I wanted to study the human body because I was interested in fashion and models. So I decided to join the life class. The class was on the top floor at the end of the building. I knocked on the door. A voice said 'Come in.' I walked into the class. I had a big heavy board with me, a new pad and new pencils. As I walked in all I could see was a group of men standing in a half- circle at least four-deep. Of course I had been locked away and I was not used to seeing so many men together. The room was completely silent. As I stepped into the room there was a nude woman posing; her breasts were hanging down towards her waist and the rest of her looked like a skinned rabbit. She was only young as well, in her 20s I would have said. I was so shocked at seeing her there and all those men that I turned around, slammed the door behind me and ran down the stairs as fast as I could go!

When I got half way down the stairs I heard a voice say 'Hello, hello, can I help you?' It was the teacher and he had obviously heard the door slam. He had a brown overall on. I thought 'Oh God, is he talking to me?' I really didn't want to know, I had never seen a nude woman before. In the home the girls had to get dressed as soon as possible and get to work, so we didn't have time to notice each other too much but this was a different kettle of fish! I said

'I am looking for the life class.'

'That's right, that's right, up here,' he replied. Little did he know that I was a novice to all of this.

I nervously went back into the room. I didn't look at the men; I just pretended they were not there. I had to walk across the room behind the nude woman to get to my seat and every eye was focused on me. I felt so embarrassed. I was looking around, fearful that I would have to talk to somebody. I was so anxious and it was so quiet in there. I got my pencils out and started sketching; I got about half of the model drawn but I didn't let anyone else see it.

At the end of the day I returned to the house and everyone wanted to know what I did at college. We giggled over it. I thought a life class was painting fruit and flowers and candles on sticks. It had never entered my head that it would be a nude woman!

I went to the class on a regular basis after that and I gradually got to sit at the front. It was a welcome outing away from the home for me. I always looked nice and took care of my appearance. There was a tea set which was fixed to a bench. We had to lean our board against the bench. Our other hand was free so that we could keep on looking and drawing. The model came and sat with me when we had a tea-break. The men had a cigarette and everyone looked at each other's drawings and eventually I gradually became used to that. I was the only female in the room – apart from the model. I suppose women didn't enrol for those classes.

It was good tuition and I was glad that I had done it because it gave me the foundation of the skeleton for when a model poses wearing an outfit. The model has to stand in certain ways. If they are standing upright they have one foot away from them at the back. The leg she is standing on should come right underneath her ear. Now, in fashion the head goes seven and a half times into the human figure and that is how you get your measurements. When you are drawing a model you can do her eight foot if you want to, which is eight or nine heads into the body. She will look really tall but it depends on what she is modelling. Then, it was the 'New Look' by Christian Dior. This style became fashionable after rationing, with short fitted and tailored tops and very full skirts. I was wearing the 'New Look'. I had a beautiful black costume with hand-embroidered pansies and saddle pockets. It was fitted at the waist and of course I had the figure for it then. It came out off the hips and there was a flared saddle on top of that with a black pencil-slim skirt; I couldn't even get on the buses it was so tight. It was down to my shins, that length was the fashion in the 1950s. I loved the fashion then and it still is an elegant look. It was a very feminine style. You saw part of the leg and the high heels accentuated the stylishness.

I went to one particular shop in Leeds when I started earning money. It sold only gloves and silk stockings. We didn't have tights then. I used to think that off-black went with everything. It was a sort of dark chocolate colour. I had high-heeled shoes on. I used to wear brogues, which I had to whiten the sides of; they were also navy blue, more like a lovely Saxe blue at the heel and the front. I wore hand-painted silk dresses and I had a beautiful French coat. I was always very fashion-conscious.

I didn't want to look like everybody else, I wanted to look different. I also had a beautiful emerald-green coat with a big collar on it. I remember even wearing a hat and the veil came under my chin and all the men were staring at me. It was the height of fashion. I had a tiny silk dress, which was flared, with white bib and buttons on it and I had a coat to go with it. Someone approached me once and asked if I was a bride, if I had just got married. I was all in pale blue and I had a pale blue hat on top of my beautiful curly hair. I wore the hat tilted on one side with a little bit over my eye and it had an ostrich feather around it the same colour as the hat. It had a 1950s fitted coat, flared at the bottom and a white silk dress underneath which was hand-painted with scattered flowers. If I had those dresses today they would be worth a mint. I always followed the work of designers such as Christian Dior and Hardy Ames. I did a drawing of Dolores with long gloves up her arm, all sleek and slender. I used my eyes and I didn't miss anything. I loved it and was doing something I really enjoyed.

One day I was walking from college back towards the home with a man who was the cartoonist for the Yorkshire Evening News. I told him that I would love to be a cartoonist because I studied people's faces and fashions and I saw some real hum-dinger faces at times. I have always had a good sense of humour as well. However, I knew what he wanted – you be nice to me and I will be nice to you darling. So he could forget it!

He was good-looking though. Men didn't leave me alone and I am not joking. It became a nightmare, it really did. Every time they saw me they thought they could chat me up and try and kiss me. I had to threaten them in the end! I was always very smartly dressed because I liked and followed the current fashion – not because I was trying to attract men!

I only saw my mum once all the time I was in the home. After I had been there for a while she was called to the home to sign some forms because I was going to be emigrating to Brisbane in Australia. I had been assigned to live with a wealthy family there. The woman of the family was a fashion designer and artist and she and her husband owned and ran a printing company. They had a big house and two beautiful children: Robin and Susan. They were looking forward to me going to live with them as a nanny for the children and to look after the house. I would have loved it.

What happened and why was I going to live on the other side of the world? The home I was living in was being closed because the upkeep costs were too high and they couldn't afford to run it any longer. All of us girls had to be placed elsewhere. So I was going to start a new and exciting life in a new country. I was delighted to think that I was at last getting my freedom and that someone wanted me – but, as usual for me, it was not to be!

This was just after the Second World War and it took nearly a year to arrange all the paperwork, visas and passport, and to book a boat passage to Australia. During that long time I had had second thoughts about moving to the other side of the world. After all, it was a huge step to make and I would have to leave my family, such as they were, and my friends in England. Also, I had started seeing my first real boyfriend, Roland, and I was still studying at art college. So my trip and resettlement in Australia fizzled out and I stayed in England.

9

Career crossroads

I really enjoyed my time at Leeds College of Art but the pattern of my life so far repeated itself. I was given hope briefly of a new life in Australia and once again it wasn't to be. After about a term and a half, Bethany House did not have the funds to send me to college any more. They were having financial difficulties and there was talk of closure.

I was still a ward of court and I was of working age so the remand home found me a job so that they didn't have to keep me. I was to work at a hairdressers' salon where I would be able to live-in. I wasn't in trouble in any way but I was put into domestic service with a miserable old woman and her husband. Their name was Mr and Mrs Flanagan and they were quite wealthy. They owned a hairdressing salon upstairs and a shop downstairs. This was in posh Headingley darling – near the famous cricket ground! During the cricket season we could see people sleeping on the pavement all night before cricket match days. They were already in the queue then waiting for tickets to the match.

The matron of the remand home thought she was sending me to a cream job – after all not everyone could say they lived and worked in Headingley! I would have preferred to go anywhere but to live with Mrs Flanagan; she was such a miserable woman. Her husband was always pleasant to me though. The wages were low and he often checked that I had some money. If I didn't have much money left from my meagre wages, Mr Flanagan asked me to run an errand for him and he gave me half a crown.

Mrs Flanagan used to say to me

'When you have had your breakfast Joan, would you come into the salon and comb my hair out? I am going out today.'

So, I went and combed her hair out and it was often on my day off! Children were treated like skivvies and we had to do as we were told in those days. We questioned nothing; we just did what we were told to do. Elders ruled! Mrs Flanagan had me sweeping and scrubbing the stairs at the front. Then I had to sweep downstairs because they had the shop, then the salon and I had to make all the girls tea and coffee. I was dictated to all the time.

I was five minutes late one night and didn't she let me know about it! I apologised and told her that the tram was delayed because it had to keep stopping. If I had walked back, I would have been later still. She said

'I am responsible for you, you will do what I say and I am not having any trouble from you.'

She was another person who didn't listen to anything I said!

While I was working at the Flanagan's hairdressing salon I was also trying to study fashion. Mrs Flanagan never let me have the light on to study. She always said she couldn't afford to have the light burning. That was how mean she was. I decorated a bedroom for her and wallpapered and painted it.

'Darling, where did you get that little treasure from?' her husband said. He added

'Let Joan do the cooking and let her make the Yorkshire puddings, she makes them better than you.'

I sat there of an evening with no one to talk to and no radio or television on. I couldn't do any drawing because Mrs Flanagan would have me shifted quicker than that. What I did wasn't important to her. I worked hard for her and I ended up doing everything. After some time I decided I couldn't stay there any longer and so I decided to move on.

I didn't return to Bethany House again because by that time it was in the process of being closed down.

After I left the Flanagan's I felt free to do what I wanted. I went into a posh large department store called Marsh & Snellgrove. It was the sort of place you only went into if you had money – rather like Harrods in London. The well-to-do ladies met up there and they had silver service dahling! So I went in and I sat there on my own. The waitress came along wearing a little black dress, with a white pinny and a frilly white hat on. She said

'Can I help you madam?'

'Yes, could I have a tray of cakes please and a cup of tea.'

Off she trotted to assemble my order. It was a lovely spacious place and I could watch everything that was going on. I felt like I was at The Ritz. I sat there drinking my tea. I didn't stare at the ladies, but I watched how their legs were positioned under the table and how the folds of their dresses fell. They were so elegant and chatted and smoked cigarettes. I just loved it! I drank all the glamour and fashion in.

I was still a ward of court and after I left the Flanagan's hairdressing salon my guardian accompanied me to a job interview as a fashion designer in Leeds. I would have to draw the models' coats and clothes and these would often be featured in fashion magazines. I didn't get that job because of my education. I truly did want to be a professional designer and artist. I had really tried to make something of my life but nobody would give me a chance.

I had to travel quite a long way from Headingley to Leeds. I caught the bus into Leeds and walked along the main industrial road with all sorts of buildings lining it and the big Leeds Fashion House. All the processes happened there: the sheep were bred in Yorkshire, the mills processed the wool and then it was dyed. Most of the women's fashions and finest suits were designed and made there. What Leeds does today London does tomorrow, and that still applies even today. All the designs and the materials came from that area as well as the designers. Many of the clothes were all ready-made so all people had to do was wear them. I followed the work of all the top designers; I was so enthralled with fashion. I studied them all – even Norman Hartnell, the Queen's designer. I was so disappointed I didn't get that job.

The only other job I went to, and which was offered to me, was in the same road. My guardian again accompanied me to the interview. She was there to support me because I was a ward of court until I reached the age of 21. We arrived at the building and it looked such a desolate place. There was ash all over the ground; the place had a rickety old wooden staircase with little paint, and grit and muck all over it. I climbed the stairs and knocked on the door. An old man opened the door and I could see behind him into the tiny room where three girls were sitting by a window. They had pots of paint on a shelf but I don't know what they were doing; I didn't get a chance to find out. I took one look inside and it looked filthy dirty.

A sort of conceited arrogance came over me and I thought 'I can't work here.' In retrospect I wish my guardian had made me stay there and told me 'You have nothing else, just stay there until something better comes up.' However, she didn't say a word. She was probably as appalled as I was and wouldn't have wanted to work in such a place herself and so she kept quiet. I could have learnt a lot there about commercial art but I suppose life had other things in store for me. My life has been like that all the way through. I have always been chasing opportunities and not quite reaching them before they are snatched away from me.

When I look back I had it all planned, with really big ideas, but it wasn't meant to be. One of the last sentences I heard my nan say was 'We should have put our Joan to dressmaking.' There was a shop in the High Street then that made wedding dresses, wedding suits and accessories. I could have been apprenticed there. What was it about me? I was so clever naturally at sewing and drawing and yet my family left me sitting on a chair at home on my own. I would have been successful at whatever I did. I was ambitious; I could have ended up being the dress designer of the shop. I could have had the dresses I designed made and put on display in the shop window. I could have done so much and now when I look back on it, I think 'What a waste of my talents. There is nothing I can't do.' However, I eventually got a job at the John Bray engineering factory in Leeds.

My very first date was with a plumber. We met in a pub opposite the Royal Theatre in Leeds. The bar was upstairs and all the stars from the theatre came in, which I thought was wonderful. While we were sitting there the pub gradually filled up and a lot of men came in. I couldn't keep my eyes off them; I have always been so curious and interested in people. I look at faces and if I see a really interesting face I keep looking, until I catch them looking back at me and then I quickly turn my head away. The men were smartly dressed and had smart suits on – and make-up! I said to my date
'Oh, aren't those men interesting?'
In fact, I was more interested in them than I was in him! He said
'Don't you know what they are?'
'No, I don't, but they look fascinating,' I replied.
He told me they were gay but I didn't know what that meant. He thought I did know and I genuinely didn't know but he had sparked my curiosity. He said
'Well, men go with men.'
'Yes, but I have women friends and we all go out together but I don't go home with them.'
That was the first time I had ever seen gay people and I thought they were wonderful. They weren't any trouble; they were handsome and laughing and enjoying themselves. I didn't care about them wearing make-up; I am an artist for goodness sake! Needless to say I only went out with the plumber once!
I met my first serious boyfriend, Roland, when I was invited by another friend to a 21st birthday party. When we started courting I was 16 and Roland was older than me. At first we got on well

together. In the end though he hurt me very much because he was so jealous all the time and I couldn't do anything. His mother was very controlling and possessive of him and I always said that if I married him I would never be able to wash and iron his shirts as well as his mother could. She brushed his clothes off after he had worn them and hung them up with tissue paper placed over them in the wardrobe. She couldn't let him live his own life and she was rather a cruel woman.

I was going to work at the John Bray factory in Leeds at six o'clock in the morning from Garforth and Castleford, which were mining towns then. I travelled to work each day with Roland's aunt Addy. We went to the market and had a big mug of tea with a bacon butty and stood in a circle eating our breakfast. Then we joined the men waiting for the bus to take us to the factory. While I was working at Bray's, and after courting Roland for a while, I moved into his mum's house so I could be nearer to him.

His mother was a tyrant and was constantly intensely jealous of me. She showed her cruelty in many ways. She had lost her little girl when she was three years old and the shock of it made her hair go white overnight. She saw a photo of Roland and me in my pocket and tore it in half. She took his half and told Roland that I had given my half to a man I was having an affair with – and he believed it! Of course I had done no such thing but it caused much friction between us. I thought she was barmy but Roland believed everything his mother said and later when we were out he nagged and nagged at me about it.

We often went to the air displays locally and he ruined the day and made me feel so miserable because he kept questioning everything I did. I ended up in tears and then I felt and looked miserable for the rest of the following week. I continued with my art and drawings but Roland was so jealous I couldn't even draw a picture of a male person. I had never heard anything so stupid in all my life!

I remember one time when I was staying at Roland's house; I had just returned from work. I went to the kitchen sink to wash my hands and in the sink there was a bucket full of water. It wasn't until I got closer to the bucket that I saw five baby kittens floating in the water! Roland's mother had drowned them. She didn't even warn me, she just left them there. It was so cruel and it shocked me so much, I felt sick. It was just another thing which pushed me away from Roland. He was so possessive all of the time, it was stifling. Roland was always so intensely jealous and he ruined our relationship and my life then. I realised that if I had married him I would have no life of my own and life would have been unbearable.

I was on the bus on my way to work with Addy and I was crying about Roland and his possessive behaviour. I told her I had to get away and that I was going to join the army. I had filled in the forms in my lunch break. Addy said

'Come and stay with me.'

Addy and I always got on like a house on fire. She knew what Roland and his mother were like. I telephoned my guardian in Lincolnshire to come and help me. I collected the few things I had and left Roland's house.

I stayed with Addy for a while and we had some laughs; we really did. We slept three in a bed. Addy was in the middle and her husband slept on one side and me on the other. We slept on a straw mattress and it was heaven to sleep on. It was snug and warm and we just sank right into it. I used to sing and we had free drinks bought for us in the pub.

Roland kept on calling for me but Addy always told him I wasn't there. He bought me a pair of boots and after I had left him his mother turned to me and said

'I will have those boots he bought you back!'

I told her she was welcome to them – and a scarf too! It broke Roland's heart when I left him. I told him he would never find a girl who came up to his mother's standards and expectations. I did portraits for him, I knitted him jumpers and I helped in the house while I was staying there. I thought 'What is it with people?' All my life I have had that.

After a while Roland changed. He had a big row with his mother and accused her of driving me away. He said to her

'It's all your fault, you have twisted my mind for me. I will marry whoever I want and I will have no interference from you, otherwise I will walk out!'

She doted on him all the time but of course it was far too late for our relationship by then.

After Roland and I separated he did eventually get married. Years later my first child was a little girl and when Roland's mother found out that I had a little girl she was so sad because she had lost her own daughter. I think losing her daughter had probably turned her mind and I felt sorry for her then. If only she had been different and hadn't been so possessive and controlling. She got jealous and resented it because he got close to me. So that was one of the reasons I joined the army. I felt free but still a bit nervous about what my future would hold.

Little did I know then that I would fall out of the frying pan and into the fire!

10

Army life and a chance meeting

I decided to join the army so that I would have a roof over my head, a good job and steady wages. I joined the Queen's Regiment and was stationed at Guildford in Surrey. I wanted to train to be a mechanic so that I could be taught to drive by the army. I thought I could become a chauffeur or drive an ambulance. There were no vacancies for drivers at the time so I had to think of another trade. I was offered a position in the stores collecting rations which meant driving to Aldershot every day. So that is what I did.

Of course at that time I was the only female in about 500 men. That was not awesome at all; it was very embarrassing because I had to climb up the steps of big army lorries with a skirt on. I used to say to the store man

'The chef in the main kitchen has run out of meat, do you think he could have some more please?'

'How much do you want my love?' the store man asked.

I only had to roll my eyes and I was given big sides of meat. Then I went to the next store

'We have run out of greaseproof paper, do you think cook could have another pack please?'

'My dear, you can have anything.'

I went back with lots of items. They had already been allocated their ration and weren't supposed to have any more but I was told 'Joan, go and help yourself to whatever is in the pantry.'

I settled into army life and one day a loud, boisterous girl came into the barracks. I thought 'Oh I hope she doesn't get the empty bed next to mine.' What happened? She came and sat on the bed next to me! Her name was Beryl. Little did I know then that she was to play a big part in my future life!

In the holidays all the lasses went home but I used to stay and talk to Beryl. I didn't have a home to go to and I just lay on my bed on Sundays. I hated Sundays. There was only the NAAFI to visit. One day Beryl said she would take me to her home but that she didn't have any money. I said

'I have money but no home.' I asked her where she lived and she said Portsmouth.

'Where's Portsmouth?' I asked.

'It's a big sea port on the south coast.' she replied.

So I paid for us both and off we went to visit Portsmouth.

Her family were renting half a house and one of her brothers walked in. His name was Raymond Jones. Beryl said

'Ray, this is my friend Joan.'

Ray shook hands with me. When I touched his hand it felt like it was a throw-back from a previous lifetime. When I look back on that I believe he was in another lifetime with me and I think he will be in a future life with me again.

Army life carried on and while I was there I was sent to the tuberculosis (TB) hospital at Hindhead for a while. I didn't have TB; I was sent there because it was thought that a relative of mine, my mother, had TB. She had been working in the clubs and apparently, while I was in the remand home, mum was very ill with TB. I knew nothing about it of course but because of that I was sent to hospital at Hindhead and that wasn't a very nice experience. I was in hospital for six weeks and I had every test available carried out to see if I had TB. One very uncomfortable experience was where fluid was drained from the lining of my stomach and tested for tuberculosis.

I had to have a further X-ray because the doctor thought he could see something on one of my lungs. The doctor told me that he had some bad news for me; there appeared to be a shadow on my lung and it would have to be further investigated, it could be TB. It turned out to be an old scar which had caused damage to the inside lining of my lung. The doctor asked if I had had a previous accident but I couldn't think why it was like that.

I had a scar on the left side of my lung which was caused years before when I was a child and my brother put a red hot poker into my back. Peter hurt me with the poker and later, when my school heard about it, they sent me to the clinic. As usual in my life, no one came to the clinic with me. When I first went there the nurse had seen a scab on my back and thought it was a carpet burn but it was actually caused by the hot poker. My brother was always a bit of a bully to me. It was an awful wound on my back and it hurt a lot at the time. I still have the scar today. I have always wondered why Peter did that to me. I don't know what I could possibly have done to provoke him.

In the TB hospital the woman in the next bed to me was married to a company Sergeant Major and I was a mere army private. Every time I turned over in bed and looked at her face we both laughed, and we laughed all day. I laughed until I was crying. We had to administer the medicine they prescribed for us ourselves and it was in castor oil – it was horrible!

The doctors eventually confirmed that I didn't have TB and I was discharged from hospital. I returned to the barracks in Guildford with a clean bill of health.

I was in the barracks having my last cup of tea of the day when a Grenadier Guard came in. I saw his uniform and said to him

'I have got a brother in the Grenadier Guards.'

He asked me where he was based and I replied that I thought he had just come back from Singapore. He told me that the unit had indeed just come back and were stationed at Pirbright in Surrey, which was not far from Guildford. He took my army number and said he would pass on my details to Peter if he saw him. I soon forgot all about it.

There was a lot of camaraderie in the army. We smoked down to the last drag of a fag and one of us would have just enough to buy a cup of tea or coffee in the NAAFI and we would all share it. A girl called Margaret became a good friend and was a big part of my life in the army. I was a big part of her life as well because the only relative she had was her dad.

That is the reason a lot of the girls joined the army; it is a wonderful institution. I loved singing and I used to be called up to sing:

'Come on Joan, give us a song.'

Then everyone else would join in, it was great fun. Margaret started courting a soldier and we all sat around the table in the NAAFI. I couldn't stand him though; he was so loud-mouthed. I suppose he was her first love but I felt she was far too nice a person for him and he seemed so rough.

I went on leave and I got severe sunburn while I was away. We would be on a charge if we got sunburn in the army because it was self-inflicted and so I had to pretend that I was sick. I couldn't go back to barracks until the sunburn had faded. I didn't intend to get burnt of course and I went to the doctor and told him I had sickness and an upset stomach so he gave me a week off work. I didn't tell him I was in the army.

After my week off I went back to army camp and looked for Margaret. I was told she had gone.

'What do you mean she has gone? She is coming back isn't she?' I replied.

'No, she is not coming back; she got married to her fella.'

I was left in complete shock; I just didn't like him, he wasn't right for her. I never saw or heard from her again. She was another person who just disappeared from my life.

One Sunday evening I went to the cinema in Guildford and everywhere else was closed. When the film finished I walked back to the camp at Stoughton Barracks. It was a fair walk from the High Street in Guildford so it took me some time. I got back and had a cup of tea from 'Smokey Joe's', which was the name of the nearby café. It had one spoon on a chain to stir your tea with. It was chained so that nobody could steal it – as if they would want that mucky, worn out old spoon!

I had to get back because my company Sergeant Major was always on her rounds with her torch making sure that no one was cavorting around the barracks with their boyfriends. When she was on duty we certainly knew it! We nicknamed her 'Ta-ra-ra-boom-de-a' because she was so loud and strict. I saw a torchlight through the bushes and it meant that Ta-ra-ra-boom-de-a was on the warpath! The MPs (military police) were out making sure that everyone was back in barracks because we would be on a charge if we were late. I started walking faster and faster until I was practically running; I didn't want to be late. I quickly removed any trace of lipstick so I wouldn't be in trouble for wearing it and I opened the guard room door.

As I opened the door into the military MPs' office, there was a big man sitting there with his feet up on the MPs' desk. I looked directly at him and I couldn't believe my eyes, it was my brother Peter! I hadn't seen Peter for four years! As he stood up I could see that he had turned into a tall young man. I was so pleased to see him that I took a running jump and dived right at him, flinging my arms around his neck. He swung me round and the girls in the office were laughing and crying. Peter had been waiting there for over two hours and the men had been entertaining him whilst waiting for me to return to camp. When Ta-ra-ra-boom-de-a came in and heard that Peter and I hadn't seen each other for years, she allowed me to have as much time with him as I wanted and she allowed me to walk him back to the bus stop.

As we were walking to the bus stop I asked Peter if he had seen mum. He said yes, he knew where mum was but he wouldn't talk about it anymore. Peter told me that he was married and had a baby daughter called Yvonne. I was an auntie! It was always my wish that if Peter had a daughter first he called her Yvonne. I liked the name because Yvonne was my best friend at school. When we parted Peter said he would come back at Easter and take me to meet his wife and see the baby. I was thrilled to bits. But Peter never came back and I didn't see him again for the next 52 years!

I stayed in the army for three years and I loved it because it became the family I never really had. I left after I got married. In those days women had to leave the services once they were married.

۶

I met my future husband, Ray, through my army friend Beryl. Ray was her brother and she had taken me home to meet her family in Portsmouth. Beryl introduced me to a tall, good-looking man with very blonde hair. He was wearing a pale blue shirt which I thought was the 'right colour' for a blonde. We shook hands and I said the daftest thing ever

'Have we met before?' I knew we hadn't met before – what a cliché! He replied

'No, I would never have forgotten you.'

He later told his mum

'I am going to marry that girl.' His mother said

'Don't be silly; she wouldn't give you a second look!'

At the time I was still in the army and I certainly wasn't ready for marriage.

After about three weeks we again visited Beryl's house and Ray asked me to go for a walk with him. I lived near the River Trent, so walking alongside the 'real' sea in Portsmouth was just breathtaking. The only thing I liked about Ray at that time was that he wasn't fresh or forward with me and he wasn't rude.

Later on Ray started turning up at the army camp during the day which caused me trouble and the MP told me to get rid of him. So I told Ray he wasn't to come to the camp gates again. He persisted and visited me a couple more times. He promised that he would stop coming if I went out with him first. We gradually got to know each other better and I started going to Portsmouth on my own. I stayed the night and slept in a room with the lady who owned the house. I used to think to myself 'Well, why aren't you at work Ray?' I told him I was not leaving the army – I most definitely wasn't! There were things I still wanted to do with the army. I was picked to go to the Cenotaph and I was looking forward to that. I had put my name down to go to the Far East and I was training for that but I didn't do either and had to give them up.

After about six months we planned to marry. When Ray first put his arms around me to say goodbye it felt as if I would never be hurt again. My head was leaning against his chest and I felt at peace and safe and I made up my mind to marry him. I did love Ray when we married but not deeply, it was more a feeling of security. The real love came later.

I had to go to court to get permission to get married because I was still a ward of court. I was 19 years old, going on 20. At that time, if you married before the age of 21 you had to get parental permission.

I didn't know then quite what an eventful and turbulent life would follow!

Raymond Jones.

11

Marrying

Ray and I got married on 3rd November 1951 at the Registry Office in St. Michael's Road in Portsmouth and I became Mrs Joan Jones. We had no money to pay for a proper reception so we bought fish and chips for supper. My army wages paid for the service. It was a sunny day and Ray's old man said 'The sun shines on the righteous.' His dad was gassed in WWI which left him with black lungs. He was tall and he suffered with asthma. He was called 'Little Samson' because he was so strong. He could pick up two men and bang their heads together. He got put in clink and thrown out of the Marines for doing that. Ray was also big; he was built like a giant. Everyone thought Ray was a weight-lifter but he wasn't. None of my family came to my wedding.

Ray wanted to go in the army but they wouldn't have him for some reason, I don't know why. I don't think he was very well educated. He was clever though and he could get a tune out of any musical instrument in minutes. If only he had had a chance. He could write and he was clever and strong. The Jones's were quite a notorious family but there was talent which was never encouraged or cultivated; it was a rough family. I had a totally different life from theirs; in my house there was always food and we were always clean. In Ray's family if you weren't there when the food was served then you went without food because someone else would eat it. The rest of his family didn't like Ray because they called him greedy over one incident. None of them had good lives. Beryl had the best life out of all of them. His sister Gwen lived in Gosport and had married a salesman and was happy enough. They had two children.

I had a long and very difficult marriage. You don't really know a person until you live with them! Ray didn't keep a regular job so my army money paid for everything at first. We didn't have a bed and so we slept on the floor with my coat rolled-up as a pillow. We went up to Leeds and stayed for a few weeks with my friend Addy. I became pregnant more or less straight away and we were living there when our first child was born, a beautiful red-haired little girl we called Yvonne.

We had been living in Leeds for about a year. Ray was coal mining and worked in the Ledston Luck (Kippax) mine but he didn't like the work. He came home from work each day black from the coal. We had a big tin bath and I had to scrub his back because the coal dust got into every pore on his body.

About three months later a house-share was offered to us. We were so pleased to move there. It was an old Victorian house and I was to look after Mr Cousens, the old man who lived there and owned the house. He had been living in the house on his own since his wife died 11 years previously. They had a daughter who had also died and so he was left completely on his own. He said he could do with a housekeeper and that we could live there rent free if I looked after the house.

I enjoyed making the home look nice. I scrubbed the front steps and window sills then donkey-stoned them which made them look smart. Donkey-stone was a soft stone which you wet and then rubbed on the front door steps. It dried to a mustard colour, only darker. I made some coloured roses from crepe paper. I had learnt to make these when I was about 13 years old. I put them in a vase I had found in a cupboard and placed them in the bay window. Everyone told the old man how lovely the front of his house looked. I loved living there.

Mr Cousins had a bed-sit in the front room with a big brass bed and heavy old furniture. One time he became very ill and kept saying he could see his dead wife and a horse and carriage. We thought that he was dying and watched over him while he rambled all night.

The next morning we called the doctor in and he told us that the old man was suffering with pneumonia. The next day Ray was at work and Yvonne was asleep in her pram. I went into the old man's room and I found him up and dressed and making a fire. He said the fire wasn't burning quickly enough and so he took out a bottle of something from a cupboard, took off the lid and started sprinkling the contents of it onto the fire. It turned out the liquid was petrol and the fire flared up so quickly that the whole house shook with the sudden impulse and the flames shot up the chimney! Mr Cousens told me he always did that to get the fire going. I was shocked and afraid of him after that and was very worried about our safety, especially with a young baby.

We lived there for six months or so and then my husband decided he didn't like living in the north. One day, out of the blue, he told me we were moving to Portsmouth. We had a baby and nowhere to live but that didn't seem to bother him; he wanted to move and what he said went!

૭

We moved south to Portsmouth and slept on Ray's sister Gwen's floor in her house in Cresswell Street. Next door there was a coal yard where horses were kept in the stables. The stables were never cleaned out properly and always smelt of urine. The business delivered coal and moved goods and furniture from one place to another. That is how they made their living.

Ray came from a big family of 17 children but not all of them lived. Ray was the third youngest. Hazel was the baby of the family but she always looked like an old lady. She went to live in Australia. Then there was Beryl who was the next daughter, Peg and Gwen. Ray's brothers were George, Sid, Leslie and Tony. All the men had genetic heart problems and were on medication.

In Portsmouth we slept on the floor on a coconut mat with our coats rolled up for pillows. The baby slept in the pram. That was until my gratuity came through from the army. I wasn't expecting a gratuity so it was a nice surprise and we were able to eat properly for a short while. I also bought pillows, blankets and sheets.

From there we went to stay in a house with the owners, Mr and Mrs Johnson. Mr Johnson was Indian and his wife was British. They were both very nice and they let us sleep on their floor. My family would have looked down at us for living like that. But my family didn't help me at all and they helped to put me on that road. I have had to survive in my life and I have had to do that the best way I could.

Ray was always in and out of work right from the start of our life together and he became selfish. My sister-in-law said to me one day

'Leave Ray because he will never change. The whole bloody family is like it. Leave while you have only got one child because if you have any more children it will get harder and harder to leave.'

My sister-in-law was right to tell me to leave Ray because I soon learnt that he would do anything not to work.

I left Ray and got a job as a live-in domestic housekeeper and one child was not objected to. The man who owned the house later got murdered! That was in Nightingale Road in Southsea, He was called Pandora and it made the front-page headlines in the Evening News.

Pandora was a business man and somebody had broken into his house. He didn't have any children and he used to feed Yvonne grapes, which he thought was amusing. He said to me

'Do you like travelling because I have got a yacht? Would you like to come across to France with me?'

I thought I had landed on my feet there but he was a big fat man and I never liked obesity. It must be from a past life that I cannot tolerate weakness. Or that is what I believed it was when I was younger. I have more compassion for it now and understand it more. I had very high ideals of how people should be and how they should behave. I hated bad behaviour and I hated obscenities. Everything had to be right.

Pandora owned an antique shop near to the sea front, in Castle Road. I spent just one night at his house, it was a Friday. His solicitor had gone into the shop to see him and Pandora told him about employing me as his housekeeper and said

'She's a lovely looking young lady with one child.'

The solicitor told him to get rid of me quick. I must not be seen there. Apparently Pandora was going through a divorce at the time and the solicitor said that his wife would take him for everything he had if she found out a woman was living there. It didn't matter what the reason was for me living there, it would go against him. So I was there for just one night. It was November and it was bitterly cold.

The next day was a Saturday and I went back to my sister-in-law's house. She was the one who suggested that I leave Ray and she was happy about me being there with her and her husband George. Ray came in on the Saturday night. He was making sounds but we couldn't understand what he was saying; we thought he was drunk. He was waving a football coupon around in his hand. His brother George looked at it and it was a £75,000 win with the penny points system. George said

'My God, you have come up on a fortune.'

The fire was blazing away and they were living on virtually nothing themselves. Ray came up to me with no animosity, put his arm around me and he said

'You can have anything you want.'

I thought yes, anything but you! I had made my mind up not to be with him and I never did anything without thinking about it carefully first.

Ray's sister, Beryl, was married to a fellow named Derek and they had split up. He was going to Germany and had come to say goodbye to us. Ray had filled the football coupon in and asked Derek to post it when he went out. Derek agreed to post the coupon for Ray. This was on a Wednesday night. The coupon had until Saturday morning to arrive. Ray eventually received a letter from the football pools company saying sorry but the coupon had arrived in the post too late and so he hadn't won anything. Derek had forgotten to post it. So we still had nothing!

Ray asked me if we could try again and said he would like a son of his own. I had nowhere to go, no money and no alternative, what else could I do? We stayed together and I fell pregnant very quickly. We went to stay with Ray's parents. They had the chance of moving a few miles away to Bedhampton into a Nissan hut. I was suffering with terrible morning sickness by then but it was nice living there with them. I gradually bought some second-hand furniture and other things to better ourselves. We never had any money really and it was always a battle to pay the 12 shillings (60p) rent each week.

Some time after that Timothy Whites, the chemist shop, had a big fire. Later Ray dug over all the debris looking for things to sell. A lot of items were buried underneath and he got hold of these and took them to the goods yard and sold them. He did this all the time I was pregnant with my second child, Keith. We were lucky if we had any food some days and some days we went without.

I had an awful pregnancy. When I was six months pregnant I got a really bad mouth infection. I went from one dentist to another in agony but no dentist would treat me. My gums were so swollen you could hardly see my teeth at all. I couldn't drink milk, I couldn't drink water; it drove me mad. I had really painful gums and as it got worse I had a mass of ulcers in my mouth. I was really ill with that and I was in such pain. There was just one dentist in Leigh Park and I knocked on his door. The dentist was not open but a young woman opened the door and I said

'Is the dentist there please because I am in agony?'

The dentist took one look at me and said

'Come in.' He looked into my mouth and said

'Oh my God!' He called in the young girl and said

'Come and see this, you may never see this again.'

It was that bad! I had something called 'trench mouth'. He said that I must have drunk from a communal cup that hadn't been washed properly and I probably wouldn't have got it if I hadn't been pregnant but because I was pregnant I was more susceptible to it. I told him I had been to see several dentists and they saw I was pregnant and the state of my mouth and wouldn't treat me. In the end it got worse and worse. He told me to see my doctor first thing in the morning which I did. It gradually improved with the right treatment.

＊

My parents-in-law were re-housed to a Nissan hut in Martin's Way, Bedhampton. There was a naval camp nearby and the Nissan huts were requisitioned after the war and used as temporary housing by Portsmouth City Council. Being a naval port, Portsmouth was heavily bombed during the war and extra housing was badly needed.

We visited Ray's parents there every Sunday. A friend and neighbour of theirs, Betty, was looking for lodgers. I was pregnant with my second child at the time and so we went to live with Betty. She had two boys and was also pregnant. It was always warm and cosy there with windows in each room. I bought two old chairs, a mat, a table and a bed-settee. All the furniture was moved by horse and cart to our new home. The hire of the horse and cart cost me 10 shillings (50p). There were fields and countryside all around us. I was happy living there and my second and third children were born there.

When Keith was born he weighed nine and a half pounds and what a beauty he was! He was six months old when I found out I was pregnant again; I was so shocked! 'I can't be. I can't be' I said. I hadn't even had chance to get over my son's birth and I had had a dreadful pregnancy. How naive can one be?

My third pregnancy was also difficult and eventually I gave birth to a lovely red-haired girl I named Marian. I was blessed because she was such a good baby. I hardly knew I had another baby. She was meant to be here.

Today I wouldn't be without all of my children – they are my whole life! I didn't appreciate that at the time when I was struggling so much but I was determined to treat my kids differently to the way I was brought up.

I had a wonderful midwife, Nurse Gunn, who was German. She

delivered Keith and Marian. I named Marian after her and she visited the posh houses all around the Havant and Rowlands Castle areas. Women had to stay in bed after giving birth in those days and I had a massive haemorrhage with Keith. I was losing my life's blood. The midwife was scooping the blood up into a bowl. I didn't realise just what was happening to me. I nearly fainted when I lay down and I started becoming confused and light-headed. The midwife couldn't telephone a doctor – mobile phones didn't exist in those days and very few people had a home telephone. One of the neighbours took Yvonne to her house whilst this was going on.

Before the midwife came I got up early and washed the kitchen floor because she was so particular. German women are like that and she was a bit neurotic. At that time I had tea chests as tables, turned upside down. I didn't have any carpets on the floors and I had two armchairs. I have had lots of problems with my pregnancies and they have affected every aspect of my life. After my haemorrhage with Keith the doctor told me not to have any more children because it could be fatal for me.

I was still on the council housing list because I always did everything the right way. Betty had her baby and came out of hospital. Betty's mother became ill and she decided she would go and live with her and look after her. Betty asked me if I would like to buy her furniture. It was heaven sent! I bought it all; carpets, furniture and her sewing machine. I had her gingham curtains with lovely little tie-backs. I paid £7 for the lot and was very pleased with the outcome. Betty was happy because she didn't have to worry about it all and so off she went to live with her mother. At the time the wages I got from Ray were £5.18 shillings (£5.18.0d) a week as a coalman. I didn't know it then, but Ray used to keep quite a lot of his wages for himself but he never gave me a penny more than the amount he thought was sufficient for keeping house and feeding us all.

I told Ray that Betty wanted £7 and I managed to scrape up a bit of money from the in-laws, a pound here and 10 shillings there. Betty did everything above-board, she had a receipt book and she signed it and put a stamp on, bless her. Years later she ended up in the workhouse with the homeless. She had a hard life and her old man treated her very badly.

I made the house as comfortable and nice-looking as I could. We had logs for the fire, it was warm and snug and we had a bathroom with a separate toilet. It was heaven-sent and was like a palace to us! The rent cost 12 shillings a week and we were very happy there – for a while anyway!

Joan and first child Yvonne.

Nissan Hut.

12

Keeping a home together

In 1944 Portsmouth City Council bought the Leigh Park Estate near Havant and planned to build a new overspill community there. After the Second World War and into the 1950s housing at Leigh Park progressed and many people were eager to move away from the slums in the over-crowded city of Portsmouth, much of which had been destroyed by heavy bombing. The Leigh Park and Havant areas were in the countryside.

I found out that Ray was going to the pub every day; I believe it was The Greyhound in Park Parade. Over a period of time Ray had been selling off our furniture until virtually all that was left were our mattresses. I was just left sitting on the only mattress we had left. He said

'You can get on with it. I am off – I have the boys at the pub to see.'

Everything was sold so that he could spend the money on drink. We had three children and barely any money for food. Ray had to be in the right all of the time and if I spoke against him he would turn violent and hit me.

I was the one who was the breadwinner in the house. I took in sewing or mending for people wherever I could and that helped to feed us. He worked for a week or he worked for six months and then he gave up his job just like that. He didn't care if there were rent and bills to pay or food and clothing to buy. He was always threatening me. I had a constant struggle to feed my kids and keep a roof over our heads and I had just had enough!

I made enquiries to move out and one day I packed a carrier bag full of clothes and other items and took my eldest daughter, Yvonne, with me. The other two kids went to stay with Ray's sister who lived nearby. I was desperate and thought that I just had to try and better my life. Yvonne could go to school and I could get a job and get some rooms and then I would get the other two children back with me. In the meantime their father could look after the two of them. He never did anything. I knew they would be well looked after by Ray's sister, Peg, because she had kids as well.

I found out about a place several miles away in Westbourne through the grown-up son of an old lady who lived there. He passed on a message to me that I could go and live at his mum's house. He was living elsewhere. So, one night while Ray was in the pub, I got myself and Yvonne ready and got on the bus. I didn't tell a soul. The other two children were already at Peg's house.

We settled into the house in Westbourne and the old lady was very kind. She seemed pleased to have someone else living in the house, especially a little girl as well. It was lovely living there. There was a back garden with vegetables growing in it. It was a nice little village and I thought nobody would know I was there. I knew that I definitely had to make the break – I just couldn't put up with any more. I continually had to start all over again. I had lost everything, all the kids' clothes, furniture, everything. The old lady gave up her bed for me and Yvonne to sleep in, bless her; I was looking forward to doing something nice for her in return.

I had been there over the weekend and on the Monday morning Yvonne went outside to play in the garden. Suddenly she came running back into the house crying

'Daddy's coming up the road!'

She was petrified. I said

'Oh my God, oh my God.'

I looked out of the kitchen window and I just caught a glimpse of Ray coming along the road – with a face like thunder! I thought 'I really am in for it now.' No sooner had I thought this than he barged his way into the house. He pushed the old gal to one side, walked in and gave me a good hiding. I fell into the fireplace. He was so strong, his hands were like shovels. The old gal got hold of Yvonne and said to her

'You tell daddy where you slept.'

'I slept with mummy in your bed and you slept in the small bed,' Yvonne replied. She was a wise old lady and was letting him know that there had been no hanky panky or other man or anything like that.

He asked me if I was going back to him. I said

'No, I am not. I wouldn't come back to you if you were the last man alive! I have had enough, everything has gone. All you want to do is go to the pub with your cronies!'

He didn't like that at all. It made him angrier to think that I had the courage to leave him and stand up to him for once. That was an awful time because then he really was on the warpath. I was scared and shaking but I stood my ground; I just couldn't take any more of him and his cruelty and abuse. I thought he could hit me as many times as he liked, I wouldn't give in. He realised then that he had lost control of me and he absolutely hated it. It didn't make any difference in the end though because Ray physically dragged me out of the house. I didn't even have time to thank the lady for letting us stay there.

The three of us got on the bus back to Leigh Park. Ray threatened me with the police because I had stolen his daughter and the Family Allowance book. I told him that it was all his doing and he deserved everything he got. I knew I would have to pay for speaking back to him like that. We were still on the bus and he was yelling at me, it was so embarrassing airing our differences in public. He always had everything. I was the breadwinner of the house. He was always threatening me – it was never-ending.

We arrived back in Leigh Park and Ray left me in the square near the blocks of flats. He yelled

'Go on, you can get on with it now! You have got no one and nowhere to live. You can just stay here!'

He walked away and I stood there stunned. I had no family to turn to. He was staying with his sister and he had Marian and

Keith there with him. I couldn't take all three children with me to Westbourne but it was the only way I could see a plan, a way out of that hell. I knew the kids would be well looked after and I knew they would be safe staying with my sister-in-law. I had just had enough and wanted revenge on him.

A friend of mine, Alice, saw me crying in the square. I still had Yvonne with me. Alice asked me what was wrong. I could barely talk to her I was so upset but I blurted out what had happened. I felt so humiliated, having to tell her that my husband had given me a good hiding, dragged me back, had threatened me with the police and God knows what and then just dumped me there. I told her that I had nowhere to go.

'Come on back to my place and have a cup of tea.' she said. We walked to Alice's flat and after a while she said I could stay there with her. I said

'How can I stay here? He will only cause problems for you.'

'He won't come here because if he does I will have the men on him,' she replied.

Alice was a prostitute but a respectable one. Prostitutes have got hearts; most of them have been driven to it for some reason and many women can understand that. In those days there was little or no help, no support from the authorities, not a thing. You just had to get on with it and survive the best way that you could. Alice was very respectable and the men loved her. I suppose a lot of the men didn't get sex from their wives and Alice didn't charge them a lot, she just tried to survive herself. She had a nice-looking, clean house. Men arrived on regular visits and I slept out of the way in the front room. They visited on a Monday evening and some were really nice fellows as well, so you couldn't really condemn them. They had their problems keeping their marriages and families together. There was always a reason; you just had to turn the other cheek and it was none of my business. I was just grateful that Yvonne and I had a roof over our heads for a while.

While I was staying with Alice, Ray got the NSPCC on to me. He had told them that I was ill-treating his kids! The man from the

NSPCC duly visited us. He could see that the children were healthy and well and so he left us alone; there was nothing to be done.

Ray came to visit me sometimes but I kept him on the doorstep when Alice was there. One day while my son, Keith, was staying with Ray's sister Peg, he came to see me. This is the part which really tore my heart in two. He was only a tot; I don't think he was even six years old. There was a tap tap at the front door. Alice was home and I opened the door and standing there was my little Keith. He said

'Hello mummy, I have come to see you.' I was choked and said

'Oh, come in darling!' I had to pretend I was alright and said

'How are you my darling, would you like a drink of milk? Come and sit down at the table and talk to me.'

I was worried that Alice would object to him being there. She didn't mind of course but that was me, I was always on edge about everything.

We sat and had our chat and he was wearing the little pullover that I had knitted for him. He looked so sweet; he had thousands of honey-coloured curls and dimples on the dearest little face. I just adored him and I still do. After a while I said to him

'You will have to go now.'

All I wanted to do was pick him up and hug him – that was the most heart-breaking time for me. He said

'Goodbye mummy, I will come again.'

How he found his way there I don't know because he didn't know where I was living.

Eventually I had to go back and live with Ray. Someone had told the authorities that I was living at Alice's house and so I was kicked out of there. The woman official who announced that I had to leave said to me

'You are a leech. You just suck up to people for your own benefit. Get out of here, you are not worthy of it! You are vermin.'

Once again I felt absolutely worthless. I was ordered to leave Alice's house by five o'clock that night.

⨎

I had been to the doctor because I had missed a few periods. I thought 'Don't tell me I am pregnant again.' Because of the upset with Ray, leaving him, living with Alice and the eviction from her place I hadn't realised that I had missed the periods but now the doctor confirmed that I was indeed pregnant once again! As the new Leigh Park estate expanded the council decided to demolish the old Nissan huts and so that meant we had to move house once more.

Ray and I went to the welfare office in West Street, Havant. I had Marian in my arms and two children, Keith and Yvonne, walking beside me. Ray was in a bad mood because he would rather have been in the pub. On the way to the office we passed a building site and all the men were working in the sunshine with their shirts off. Suddenly Ray grabbed hold of my long hair and jerked my head back. He shouted out to the men

'Anyone want a go with her? Come on, I will give you chance to, make your offer now.'

It was so humiliating and I just sobbed my heart out. The men just went quiet; I think they couldn't believe what they were seeing and hearing. Ray was such a big man; no one would want to tackle him. I felt degraded and worthless yet again.

When we arrived at the welfare office I was still crying. I was in such despair because I had no family of my own to stick up for me. It has always been like that all my life. I have always been accused of things I haven't done and nobody ever wanted to listen to me. In the office I was sitting crying and cuddling Marian. Mrs Linguard was the Welfare Officer and she dealt with broken homes and families. She could see the bruises on my arms and the lump on my chin. She said sternly to Ray

'YOU, you stay there; I will deal with you later!'

Mrs Linguard took me into her office, offered me a cigarette and gave me a cup of tea. She said

'Tell me what happened dear.'

In between sobs I told her that he had thrown me out and hit me. She called Ray into the office and said

'YOU did this to your wife and because of the way you have treated her, I am going to get the law onto you!'

She got straight on the phone and called the Clerk of the Courts. The Court office was nearby. She said

'Would you come over here and read this man his rights please because he has been beating up his wife?'

The clerk came straight over. The clerk looked at Ray and said

'I know you. You are one of the Jones's and you have been trouble ever since you have been in Portsmouth. You are a big family as well.'

Ray couldn't deny it and he was as meek and mild as you like in front of both of them. The clerk read Ray his rights and said

'If we find out that you have touched this lady, your wife, one more time I will have you quicker than that and you will go straight to prison. I will make sure that you do!'

After that, the awful thing was they persuaded me to go back to Ray! Mrs Linguard wanted to talk to me on my own again. She said

'Look, he obviously wants you back; would you go back to him?'

'You don't know what you are asking me, I hate him, I hate him! I am ashamed of him. I don't want to go back. I don't want him touching me! He has never cared for me. He has given me all these kids and then left me to fend for myself. I am nothing but a slave!'

I had always covered my true feelings up, put on a smile and got on with life. I did everything I possibly could. My kids always looked nice, I made all their clothes out of second-hand clothing and I kept my home as clean and nice as I could. It felt like my childhood starting all over again. This time though I did speak up, I just couldn't take any more! I was bruised and in pain, I had a lump on my chin and a red mark on my face. I told her that I had left him and it was time for me to make a new home with my children.

13

Housing crisis

The council moved all the families living in the old Nissan huts, except our family, to an area which was opposite the huts. There were some new houses being built near the new Curlew pub. I was one of the last people the council saw so instead they sent me to St. John's Road in Bedhampton. I didn't want to move, I felt a great foreboding and seemed to sense that it would all go wrong there – and it certainly did!

While we were living at the house in St. John's Road I gave birth to my fourth child, Stephen. He was the most beautiful baby. He had the biggest blue eyes you have ever seen and he was such a happy baby; he really was adorable. My other three children were still quite small and now I had three in a pram.

Ray began work sand-blasting on the Hayling Island Bridge, where the old Hayling Billy railway line used to run. He earned really good money for a while and then the job finished so he was out of work again. He sometimes found an odd week's work here or there but if he didn't like the job he wouldn't go back. I had made a lovely home by then but Bedhampton was an expensive area to live in. Ray was out of work; we got into arrears with the rent and so we were evicted.

We had been saved from eviction once before by the SAAFA organisation, the armed forces charity. I was in the army for three years and SAAFA settled the eviction order and paid the rent. Life went on and Ray wasn't even trying to find work so we soon got back into arrears with the rent again. We were served with another eviction order and the bailiffs turned up with a big lorry accompanied by the police! Everyone in the street respected me and I didn't want people to see me being evicted – what a humiliation! I woke the children up early and got them dressed. They were so good; they never asked what was happening or cried. They just did what I asked them to do. They seemed to just know. I had made a lovely home by then but I had to sell what I could and walk away with just a few carrier bags of clothing and three kids; Yvonne, Keith and Marian.

Ray's sister Beryl had come to see me the day before we were evicted. No one in the family came forward and said

'Look, how much do you owe for goodness sake? I will loan you the money.'

While Beryl's husband was away at sea she had gone out on a date with her friend Peter Arnett. The Arnett's owned fisheries in the Portsmouth area and had a lot of money. Beryl was attractive with honey blonde hair and while her husband was away she and Peter went up to London to see a big boxing match. On the way home they had a car crash and hit a bridge wall. Beryl hit the windscreen but wasn't seriously hurt. She had a cut across her nose and had torn ligaments in her leg and one or two other scratches. She received £1,000 compensation after the accident.

Beryl came to me and said

'Let me have the baby. I have had this accident and looking after Stephen will help me to get over it.'

She couldn't have any children of her own then but she did end up with two daughters several years later. I very reluctantly let Steve go, and only because the authorities had threatened to take all my children away from me. So it seemed to make sense at the time. I had four children and nowhere to live. I thought Steve would at least be well looked after with a roof over his head, be well fed and be doted on by his aunt. I would get him back as soon as I found somewhere else to live. I had a nasty, horrible gut feeling about it. I must have sensed something all those years ago when I first met Beryl in the army barracks although I didn't know then what the future held for us.

So, I very reluctantly handed Steve over to Beryl intending it to be for a short while until things had settled down and we were re-housed. The awful thing is that I never got Steve back. I think I must have had the devil sitting on my shoulder laughing his head off!

We eventually found somewhere else to live and every time I went to Beryl's house to get Steve back he was sat there in a big Princess pram looking happy and healthy and with all the latest clothes and toys. He was a picture of health and he looked just adorable. He was clean, well fed and happy and Beryl absolutely doted on him. It made me ill and I didn't have the heart to take him away from her so I broke my own heart. I gave in to her; she could give him everything that I couldn't. He would have a better life with Beryl.

Steve left her when he was 15 because he grew to dislike her. She took him to Australia to live and they were there for three or four years. She sent me photographs of him. She eventually had two girls of her own and I think because she had her own children Steve got pushed aside. She shouted at him and their relationship turned bad. Steve has since said to me

'You did what you had to do and you gave me a good home.'

14

Moving from house to house

After the eviction we stayed with Ray's sister, Peg. Peg lived near Havant and she asked if I would go to court with her as her husband was there for non-payment of rates. He was put in prison for two years so my sister-in-law asked us to live with her. Two years in prison for non-payment of rates!! That would be unheard of now. The authorities make a deal with you these days to pay so much a week but you don't go to prison. Because Peg's husband was in prison the welfare didn't want to give her any money. She would have been in trouble if the council had found out we were living there because we had been evicted. Peg's mother was also living in the house and we all helped each other wherever we could. Peg didn't want to be on her own. So we moved once again and for a while we were happy there.

At the time Peg was pregnant and I was also pregnant yet again. I only ever knew I was pregnant at the fourth month, I had periods before that. I nearly killed myself trying to terminate an earlier pregnancy. I used a syringe and had a miscarriage at four and a half months. I had a haemorrhage and I ended up in hospital. That was ignorance on my part. My friend had come to visit us with her husband and he said to Ray

'What's the matter with Joan? She looks a bit down in the mouth?'

I had just realised that I was pregnant again and I thought 'Oh God, this will be my fifth child, when is it going to end?' I wanted a better life for me and my kids. I felt in quite deep despair at the time, I felt worn out, exhausted. Another friend's husband told us that his wife had missed one period and she had used a syringe with soapy water and douched herself and later she had a period. It sounded quite easy and I really didn't know what I was doing but I was desperate so I tried using the syringe. I didn't really think it would work on me. Nothing happened so later that evening I went up to bed.

I woke up at 4 am to use the toilet. I had taken a bucket up to bed with me just in case something happened. When I sat on the bucket I felt something come away. I felt terrible. I was shaking and feeling hot and cold. I had to keep Yvonne home from school later that day to look after me. I didn't dare tell a doctor because I knew I would get myself into trouble. Trouble seemed to follow me from one thing to another. In the end I was haemorrhaging and at about 2 o'clock in the afternoon I said to Ray

'Get the doctor! Get the doctor quick!'

I felt as if I was going to collapse.

Ray called the doctor in to me. The bucket was full of blood. The doctor sat on the bed and put his hand into the bucket to see if I had lost anything. I knew I had lost something but didn't know what. The doctor said

'It looks as if you have lost half your blood and you will have to go into hospital and have a blood transfusion.'

He asked me if I had taken anything. Of course I told him I hadn't taken anything – just a couple of tablets – but I didn't think they had any effect. I didn't dare tell him I had used a syringe.

Once I was in the hospital the other half came away. The doctor said that I had been very lucky and that if I had waited another 24 hours septicaemia would have set in and I would have died! I had a blood transfusion and eventually returned to Peg's house.

Life carried on and some time later I gave birth to another child, another lovely little girl we named Sheree. My sister-in-law gave birth to a boy around the same time. She was pregnant when her husband was sent to prison. When he came out of prison he wasn't very nice to us and he didn't want us living there anymore. What my husband and I didn't know was that Peg was in arrears with her rent and had a notice of eviction herself.

We weren't supposed to be living with another family but because Peg's husband was not there it was alright. The housing people came to the house one day. I happened to be out and Ray was at work. As I was walking along the road I saw Peg standing at the front door. There was a man holding a clipboard standing there with her. I thought it would be best if I kept out of the way. If I had walked into the house the authorities might have found out that my family was living there. Peg swore blind that we weren't living there. They weren't making trouble for her; they just wanted to know who was there because Peg was going to be evicted.

Peg was evicted and of course that meant we were also homeless – again! Peg's youngest sister and her husband came and collected Peg's family up and took them back to their house. They never said a word to me, they just left us all. I was in a real dilemma then because I was pregnant once more!

The next day I went to see the housing people because I was still on the housing list. A young man sitting at the desk in the housing office accused me of lying. He said

'Why would the lady living there tell a lie and say that you were definitely not living there and you are saying you were?'

I told him we had been living there for the last two years while her husband was in prison! I told him that we had both been pregnant at the same time and had our babies together. I said she was frightened of getting into trouble because by rights we shouldn't have been there.

'You are a liar, you are a liar' the man said.

Ray was standing there with me and he didn't say one word. The man said

'If I catch you outside with that baby in your arms I will have all your children taken away from you!'

We didn't have anywhere to go, not then. The young man in the housing office had a girl sitting with him during the interview and he was trying to show off his authority in front of her. I thought that the girl could have done something because I was really pleading with them and eating humble pie. I was desperate! Why did it always have to fall on me to sort out? It was never Ray who saved us, it was always me.

I had four children with me at the time. We didn't have anywhere at all to go. Peg's next door neighbour said to me

'My daughter is staying with me because her husband is away in the navy, so here's the key to her house, you can stay there temporarily. I have a mattress and you can sleep in the living room and use the facilities'.

I have always been well liked and some people did show some compassion towards me then. All I had was a few paper carrier bags with what clothes I could carry in them. I had to leave everything else behind, even the kids toys, everything.

We stayed at the house for two nights and then we went to see the housing people again and I explained exactly what had happened. I saw different people the second time. Within a fortnight I received a letter from the housing office and I went down to see them. They gave me the keys to a house in Cranleigh Road in Portsmouth. I was expecting the house to be in Leigh Park but it was miles away in Portsmouth – but I was grateful because it was somewhere to live.

We stayed for one night with my husband's youngest brother before we moved into the house in Cranleigh Road. I had a broom and a pram and nothing else. So I had to find second-hand carpets, furniture, beds, etc. Even though everything was second-hand it cost us a lot but somehow we managed. We lived there for the next 15 years. I did have threats of eviction during that 15 years and the threat of eviction is dreadful when you have a family. It adds years onto you.

We collected the keys to the house in Cranleigh Road, and I loaded up the old pram with a sweeping brush, Fairy Liquid, second-hand saucepans and cloths for cleaning. It was the end of being homeless – wow!! To have that roof over our heads meant

everything. My youngest child had just started walking then. We could start a new home – once again. Everything we had for our new home was second-hand.

The kitchen was awful. It had a shallow sink with a tap which was high up on the wall and splashed everyone who tried to use it. Rafters were showing through the ceiling in places and there was an outside toilet. The kitchen wall was only four inches thick and when it rained outside we had dampness on the inside. When I cooked, the condensation made the walls so damp and whatever I did to try and improve it made no impression on it. We just had to live with it and took it in our stride. It was somewhere to live.

Ray used to make me go to the welfare office in North End to ask for money. He badgered me to go there, it was so embarrassing. I had never had to beg for anything before. The people in the office said things like

'Oh, you are here to tell a few more lies are you? Where is he, hiding behind your skirts?'

I used to think to myself this is my husband you are talking about. I did have a little respect for him at the time but I hated it, hated it. When I came back with nothing I got it in the earhole from Ray. He ranted at me

'Why haven't you got anything?'

He just wanted tobacco or beer money. Everything was always my fault and I learnt to accept it. At that time I wouldn't have received any help if I had walked away either.

It was hard not having enough money to go and buy decent things for the home, but I have always had a good eye and knew a good thing when I saw it. I was clever with my hands too and so I set about cleaning windows and washing floors. I put up with second-hand curtains and hoped that they looked nice; what else could I do? Only wait until I could better them. I had a toasting dish which had a handle, so I put some chips in the 'old oven' hoping they would cook for the children. When I took them out of the oven the handle had melted and fell on my foot. So now, on top of everything else, I had an injured foot.

We acquired a television, which was something, but when we all sat down to watch it we couldn't get a picture and we were so disappointed. There was no aerial and we didn't know then that a bent coat hanger would have done the job as an aerial! We didn't have many covers for the beds. I was told that there was a shop in Arundel Street where you could get feather quilts and you could buy pieces from old quilts when they were sent there for re-covering. So, with my family allowance I went there and for six shillings I came away with a lot of different materials and some were lovely satin pieces. I sat and stitched them all together. It took a reel of cotton to make one quilt but they did look lovely.

I needn't have bothered with all that but I wanted my children and my husband to have nice beds to sleep in. I didn't possess a thimble and so I ended up with a hole in my finger from continually pushing the needle into the material. I was always on the lookout to better my home. I re-covered chairs, made curtains, took up someone's trousers or put a zip in a skirt. My work brought in a few shillings to buy bread or potatoes, it all helped.

I became pregnant again, which I just hadn't bargained for. I had wanted to get a job and earn some money but now I was tied down again. The contraceptive pill wasn't widely available in those days and people looked down on us because we were a big family. I found out I was four months pregnant; once again I hadn't noticed that my periods had stopped. How could I? I was so busy I didn't realise. All I could do was grin and bear it.

15

Working all the hours

I was trying to cope for a long time and I became angry with God. Too many times I had just managed to scrape together enough food for a meal for us all. Keith had a bicycle given to him by a neighbour and he went out and sold it. He was so thrilled to come back with the money for me; he only kept a couple of shillings out of it. He was always so thoughtful and caring. He always did everything he could for me and he was no age himself. I could never have afforded to buy him a bike. He didn't tell me what he was doing. One Saturday morning I told him

'Don't ask me for ice cream, I don't even know where I am going to get a dinner for today.'

The kids always understood when I said we can't do this or that. Not one of them rebelled against it; they were so good.

One particular day the children were at school and I got very angry. I was sick of constantly worrying about money to buy food and pay the rent. We were getting into arrears with the rent and it was escalating once again. I was working at home, mending clothes, taking in sewing and getting a pittance for it but as long as I could buy a loaf of bread and some milk I could feed the kids. I was lucky if I got £5 for taking up a pair of trousers, a skirt or a dress. I was also working at cleaning and scrubbing floors. People often said to me

'I don't know how your kids look so clean and smart when they step outside the door.'

I made them waistcoats and dickie-bow ties. Their shirts were made out of a man's shirt. I could make pyjamas out of men's shirts, they always looked smart. I had to boil up water for the baths in that crummy, awful little kitchen because we didn't have a bathroom. You couldn't really call it a kitchen; there were no cupboard units in there. I just had a sideboard and a shallow sink, a dreadful tap and a ghastly old cooker and that was it. I never had anything bought for me.

Too much money went into the pub and if I dared to try and stop it I didn't only get it but the kids got it as well. I was fed up with continually slaving away. I did the cleaning, prepared and put the dinner on, bathed the kids, shampooed their hair, polished all the shoes and made sure they all looked clean and tidy before they left the house. We were a big family but that wasn't their fault. That's how I looked at it. So whatever it took, I did it.

I had heard Mrs Smith, who lived across the road, was unwell so I asked one of the kids to knock on her door and ask her if she wanted any shopping done at the butcher's shop or the Post Office. Very often they ran round to the Spar shop and got something for her. I said to them

'When you have given Mrs Smith the shopping, do not hold your hand out for anything, you will learn to do it for nothing.'

They all remember that and say you did so much for us and we are all good people.

The kids had only one pair of socks each and I just couldn't get them white any longer. I got very angry and I said out loud

'There's him, he spends all that money in the pub and the kids need new shoes, they are nearly worn through.'

It was a blessing when summer came because they could wear sandals. I was worn out and very angry saying

'That's it God, I am wiping my hands of it all now. I do the best I can with everything. I make the kids clothes, I teach my kids to be good and to always tell me the truth and I deal with it. I teach my kids to do good turns for other people and not expect anything in return but no one does me a good turn! All I always seem to get is the scrag-end of everything. All I have is nothing but worry and all the hard work to go with it. My girls have got one pair of knickers and one vest each, and grubby old socks which I have to boil up in a big copper pot.'

(The pot weighed a ton and came from a second-hand shop.) I didn't have a washing machine; I had cold water and an outside toilet. I said

'All of my friends have got washing machines, hot water and bathrooms and I feel ashamed sometimes when my friends come to visit me. I just have to grin and bear it and make out that everything is fine.'

I had a lot of kids and my husband would not take no for an answer. He kept me awake all night until eventually I had to give in to his demands. People said

'Oh, you are not having another baby are you? You don't want any more do you?'

'Yes, of course I do. I want another half dozen!' I used to reply.

I carried on ranting to God

'I have had enough now, I am not teaching my kids anything more, it doesn't get me anywhere, nobody helps me and I have no family I can turn to.'

That's just how it was for me and I really did let rip. I felt so angry and in utter despair! I really didn't expect anything to come of it.

I went to my brother-in-law Tony's house in Leigh Park. The kids loved going there because Tony had a big family and all the children got on well together. Tony was Ray's youngest brother. They really loved each other and were the best of friends as well as brothers. Tony adored me. He said to Ray

'If I had been a little bit older you wouldn't have stood a chance, I would have married her.'

He always said that, right up until he died. We all got on so well. Sometimes we spent the night there. All the kids tucked in with each other.

We returned from Tony's the next evening about seven o'clock. It had been snowing and our two bottles of milk were still on the front doorstep. The ice had made the cream rise up under the tin foil bottle top. I pointed it out to the kids and as we were looking at the milk a woman I knew walked up to our house. I said

'Hello Dot, what are you doing here?'

'Oh, I just thought I would come round to see you.' she replied. It was seven o'clock in the evening and I said

'It is late and you never come around here at this time. What is going on?' I invited her in for a cup of tea and I put the kettle on. The kids had had a bath at Uncle Tony's and were ready for bed so I sent them on up to bed.

We had a cup of tea and Dot said

'I expect you are wondering why I have come to see you? You know you do two shillings on the Cancer Football each week? Well, your numbers have come up and this is *your* money – and not his!' She knew that it would go in the pub if Ray got hold of it. Dot passed me a brown envelope and said

'It is not a fortune but it will help you.' There was £33 in the envelope! I gave her the £3 for her trouble and she was grateful. I thought that was fair. I said

'Oh, wonderful, tomorrow I can go into town and buy some new white vests and socks for the girls and get some socks for the lads'.

I had spent the whole £30 in my mind. It didn't go far but it got me that and I was very grateful for it. That wasn't all!

At that time Ray was doing casual work for Bill Clements, the coalman. It was a big family-run coal merchants business. Bill fetched Ray's orders to our door. Monday morning came and before I had got myself ready to go and buy the new clothes for the children, my old rent man was at the door. He was a lovely old man. He always had a dew drop on the end of his nose and it was a real bony nose, like a pointed beak. His face was full of character, I could have drawn it. He was thin and he wore a grey gabardine mack and had his notepad in his hand. We exchanged polite greetings to each other. At least he treated me like a human being!

He said

'It is not a very nice morning but I have some good news for you. I don't know how it happened but we have been charging you too much rent.'

I looked up towards the sky and said

'Thank you.'

'I can't give it to you in cash but what it will do is it will take off your rent arrears of £11.22 and it will also pay your rent for the next three weeks.'

Well, that was as good as a bar of gold to me! So that was surprise number two. I thought 'Oh, it would only take Ray to get a permanent job and if only Bill Clements would knock the door and say "Bring your cards in Ray and we will take you on permanently"'.

It turned out to be quite an eventful week for me. At the end of that week Bill came to the house to deliver Ray's wages to him. They spoke about the day's events and just before Ray closed the door Bill said

'Oh, by the way Ray, fetch your cards in on Monday and we will take you on permanently.'

I was astounded! I said to God

'I am so sorry, I will never do it again. You have answered my cry for help with all that I wanted.'

I didn't realise it then but that was my first ever real-life manifestation. I was manifesting by asking. I do say to people, as it is in the Bible, and it stands today: 'Ask and it shall be given.' You just need to ask from the heart and if you have real feeling and it is not for yourself, it will happen. It was for my kids and to keep a roof over our heads.

So you can see how my life has gone.

Four children: Keith, Yvonne, Marian and Sheree.

121

16

Blessings and a curse

After I had given birth to my sixth child, Graham, I tried hard to be sterilised because I could see that I would go on and on being pregnant and Ray didn't seem to care. He was still spending all our money in the pub and spent most of his time there. I was 29 then and the doctors wouldn't sterilise me because they said I was too young. I explained to them that in 10 years' time I could have another five or six children and my husband was only on the wages of a common old lorry driver and that wasn't enough money to keep us even then.

The doctors didn't care at all. As far as they were concerned, *they* thought I was too young but they didn't look ahead or take into account the number of children I already had and our circumstances. It was all very well men talking to women like that but they didn't have the children and the worry about the care of them, they could just walk away from it. Women were expected to do as they were told, the husband was in charge! Men ruled in those days.

I had two miscarriages earlier and with one of them the baby had died at four and a half months. It had mortified and septicaemia had set in. I knew that something wasn't right and I felt really unwell. The doctors kept saying that I wasn't pregnant and I kept saying 'There is something wrong with me.'

Eventually I had a miscarriage. The foetus had managed to work itself away. There were bits of bone and flesh and the doctor wouldn't believe it when Ray explained what had happened. I was half-way through this pregnancy and I was rushed into hospital. The doctor told Ray that if I had left it any longer I would have been dead. It made me realise just how near to death a person can get. Sadly, altogether I have had three miscarriages.

In 1964 I became pregnant again with my last child, Diane, and I had a threatened miscarriage. I fell down the stairs in my house from top to bottom. How I didn't lose my baby I will never know. I hurt my back when I hit the bottom step and I had terrible backache and felt ill. I went to see my doctor who told me that I had placenta first and that I was to go straight into hospital because the condition was dangerous. The placenta became lodged underneath the baby, probably due to the fall, and I could have haemorrhaged and died at any time if I had gone into labour.

I wouldn't go into hospital until everything was alright at home. I had to get on my sewing machine and make three pairs of school trousers for the boys. The specialist asked if I had any of my own family who could help me. I said no, there was no one who could look after me and my kids. He told me to go into hospital immediately. I should have gone to hospital there and then but my friend was waiting outside the surgery in her car for me and I had to sort my children out at home first. I couldn't rely on Ray for support.

I went into hospital a couple of days later and I was there for seven weeks. The doctors told me the baby would be tiny, only about four pounds. My beautiful Diane weighed six pounds when she arrived. I came out of hospital in the afternoon and I was alright that night. The next morning Ray had gone to work and at three o'clock in the afternoon I was still in my dressing gown. The kids were in the garden playing. Ray was like a sergeant major with the kids and used them like slaves, ordering them about, making them clean windows, polish the furniture and do various other chores. He sounds like an awful man but he did have a few good points as well. If he had money in his pocket he lined all the kids up and told them that whatever money they asked him for he would give them. They loved that game.

The doorbell rang and I answered the door to a bald-headed man who was wearing a raincoat and holding a clipboard. He came into the house and sat at the kitchen table. He said

'Right, I am here because I want to know the age and sex of all of your children because I have to find homes for them. Due to non-payment of rent you are going to be evicted and your children are going into care.'

I had a thumping headache and I started crying; I just couldn't talk to the man, I felt devastated. I had had an awful time with my pregnancy. I had to have an emergency operation in hospital because I had placenta first and had gone into labour. I was recovering from that and this was the one thing I was afraid would happen. All the weeks I was in hospital I kept asking Ray if he had paid the rent each week. He assured me each time he had paid it and said

'Of course I have paid the rent. What do you think I am going to do, not pay the rent while you are in hospital?'

Every time when this sort of thing happened I had to face the authorities, it always dropped into my lap. Why did Ray never have to face them?

It was a bright sunny day and Keith came running into the house and got himself a drink of water from the tap. He was out of breath and he turned to look at me, although I tried my hardest not to look at him. He could see I was distressed and he came up to me, put his arms around me and said

'Mummy, is this man annoying you?'

I don't know what he thought he was going to do about it though. I said

'No, of course he is not darling, you go out to play. Mummy has just got a real bad headache and I haven't slept very well.'

So off he went and he didn't know any different.

I gave the man all the information he needed. He must have thoroughly enjoyed his job because he had no sympathy at all; no compassion and I thought

'You have got the job you deserve, watching people in absolute misery.'

I said to him

'By the way, there is a new-born baby upstairs.'

'Oh I wondered why you were in your dressing gown at three o'clock in the afternoon,' he replied. That was his whole attitude!

When Ray came home later that day I told him what had happened and I said to him

'How many times did I ask you if you had paid the rent?'

'Look, I couldn't go to work while you were in hospital and leave a big family. What was I to do in a situation like that? If I had gone to work I would have had to leave the kids on their own all day in the house.'

I understood the logic of that and thought oh well, so be it, we will have to deal with this now. I told him that we were definitely going to be evicted.

&

I decided I would write a letter to the council. I wrote a long two-page letter and I poured my heart out explaining what kind of a father could leave a large family of children at home all day while he went to work and his wife was in hospital in a life-or-death situation? I didn't have any option but to go into hospital. I came out of hospital the day after my daughter was born. We didn't have any money coming into the household so my husband couldn't pay the rent. It was weekly wages in those days.

I said I felt that I was the one who was being victimised, also my children, and we didn't deserve this threat hanging over us while I was trying to recover from an operation and my long stay in hospital. It wasn't easy, I was bleeding all the time and I had really worried about what I would be giving birth to. It was awful. I felt like I was being punished for having a baby and yet it was out of my hands. I couldn't say no to Ray, he would never take no for an answer, he was too big and strong. He had a 'no woman says no to me' attitude and 'nobody tells me what to do either, I will do what I want to do.' He always bullied me into it.

It was very much a man's world then. Men pleased themselves and the women had to toe the line and get on with it. That was how it was in those days: men had all the good jobs. Women didn't go out to work so much, they stayed at home and looked after the children. Men earned the wages and most of them doled out to the women so much each week for rent, food, clothing and school dinner money. Women were definitely considered the weaker sex and had to obey their husbands, they had no say in most matters. It is so very different today and it is difficult for young people to understand what it was like then. Now we have more equality between the sexes; women are independent and most have careers and well-paid jobs.

I received a letter from the council saying they were going to make a decision and I was to telephone them on a certain day. I rang a Mr Dant, who was very kind and was the Housing Manager at the council at that time. He said

'Mrs Jones we are letting you have the keys back, you can stay there and you will not be evicted.'

I was so relieved. It was my letter to the council which sorted that particular crisis out for us.

Three months later, when Diane was three months old, Ray forced me to go out and clean the pub where he went drinking. He told me I had to go because he told them that I would and he didn't want to lose face with his friends – cheek! I had five children at home and one in the pram. I had to take the baby with me because Ray didn't look after her and yet he was only around the corner. I never forgave him for that because it was bitterly cold that winter; her little hands were purple and she was crying.

I was livid with him! He was sitting there drinking and looking at my backside while I was scrubbing the floor! I could feel his eyes on me. If I had been a man I would have hit him good and hard! I have always had a happy temperament but he created such alien and bad feelings in me at times.

Another time I got a job in the Radical Club and I scrubbed the dance floor every day of the year, Christmas morning as well. Diane came to work with me right from three months old up until when she started school at five years. The landlady's small son and Diane used to play together. They had a bucket on wheels and took it in turns; one to sit in it and the other one to push it round, making more marks for me to clean. When I got home again I was very tired because then I had to do all the washing by hand and the cooking. I didn't have a washing machine until many years later.

From then on I continued working until my lovely daughter started school at five years old. She came with me every day, Easter, Whitsun, Christmas, all the time. All the money I earned had to stretch to everything; all Ray paid for was the rent. He asked me on a Saturday night to hand over my money but I hid it so he couldn't have it. I needed it to buy food and clothing and pay the bills. He got angry and he often found it and spent it in the pub. The children sat on the stairs and listened and came down to me after he had gone out.

One day, I tried to get him up to go to work and I called him again and again. I took him up a cup of tea in bed to wake him. I knew he would lose the job if he didn't get up. He started to get out of bed with his fist held up ready to hit me. I stood my ground and said

'Go on then, hit me, I am just your size.'

He shot out of bed and went to the wardrobe, got out my few clothes, grabbed my arm and threw me down the stairs. He threw my clothes out onto the pavement and shoved me out with them. I grabbed everything up and hoped that no one would see this going on; then I walked to work.

At work I started scrubbing the floor; it was a dance floor so all the scuffs had to come off. I couldn't stop crying, I was so unhappy and was worried about the children. No one wants you when you have problems. I felt so alone and had no one to turn to.

It was very difficult and hard work having a big family, one after another and all too often being the main bread-winner! Again I tried to get sterilised but the doctors said I was too young to have that procedure. That was at St Mary's Hospital. I told them I wanted to give some quality to my family but they still said no! Of course the doctor was a male! It seems that women aren't responsible enough to make those decisions. At least they weren't then in the 1950s and 60s. So, I just had to get on with it and do the best job that I could. I was always worried that I could become pregnant again. There wasn't enough money to go round. It was a constant struggle.

Sometimes I looked around to see what I could sell: white cotton, out-grown clothes. It was only ever a small bundle. There was a rag and bone merchants near where we lived. I sent a couple of the children to take the bundle and if they came back with money we could have dinner that day. It always made me feel grateful for what we had and the love I have always had for my children helped a lot. They never complained and my life without them wouldn't have been much.

We only had a cold water tap with one cupboard to keep everything in and we had a miserable old cooker. We had an outside toilet and no bathroom, just a tin bath which I had to buy, of course! It was second-hand but I was so grateful to have it. After all, the children had a bath, which I had to keep topping up with hot water. My son and I carried this heavy tub out of the back door, which wasn't easy because we had to turn it at an angle to get it in and out of the door. The water 'slapped around' in the tub and we laughed.

I said to my son

'Let's be as quiet as we can.'

I didn't want the neighbours to know. Next morning the children asked me where the soap had gone. In the garden I expect! Ha Ha. We always had a giggle when it was not expected.

Feeding the children was difficult. The more children I had the more I had to spread things out to make them go round, but I always managed. It's surprising what you can do with half a pound of mincemeat. I made dumplings to go with it. We had stew, with lots of vegetables and Yorkshire pudding. I always made a sweet of some sort; rice or steamed Golden Syrup pudding. My kids rarely went hungry.

We lived in the house in Cranleigh Road for 15 years and during that time I tried to improve life and put in for a house transfer. Two Council men came in dressed wearing smart suits and asked where I would like to live. I was offered a three-bedroom house on a Paulsgrove estate, north of Portsmouth. I declined that house because at that time the area made the headlines in the local newspaper because of the activities of gangs. I was offered another house in the extreme north of Portsmouth. Again, I thanked them but declined and decided to stay in the Cranleigh Road house.

Before they left I invited them to look at my kitchen. We had worms coming up through the hard flagstone floor, there was no ventilation or air bricks in the kitchen and the walls were thin, so condensation was always running down the walls. We had a low-down sink and a high cold water tap so when the tap was turned on water splashed everywhere. After their visit I was repeatedly offered flats but I just couldn't go into a flat with a big family of children of all ages. It would have been dangerous but they didn't seem to understand that. I still earned a little money which often kept us from starvation. Maybe five shillings for taking up curtains, 10 shillings for taking up turn-ups on new trousers. I made a cape for the daughter of a friend and made alterations for a lot of people's clothes.

Things settled down for a while and one day I was talking to my next-door-but-one neighbour and during the conversation she asked me how much rent I paid each week. She knew we were living in a council house. I told her how much I was paying in rent and she said

'You get down to that council office tomorrow and offer to buy the house because that is what I did and I am now paying half that amount. Hurry up and get down to the office because they are going to change the law.'

I was so excited at the possibility of improving my life that the very next morning I went straight to the council office and enquired about buying the house. The woman at the housing office said

'I am so sorry my dear, it has been announced in the newspaper today that the council has now stopped selling its houses.'

I was so disappointed that I had only just missed yet another opportunity to better myself and my family. Why have these chances always been denied to me in life? Life was always a struggle, living a difficult and precarious day-to-day existence.

When the children were growing up they were becoming more independent by the day! On a Sunday, when their dad was getting ready to go out to the pub, which didn't open until 7.00 pm in those days, the kids were bathed, hair washed and I said

'Come on then, up to bed all of you.'

They went upstairs and when their dad closed the front door, they came running down the stairs again. It was our time for fun! The little one put my tights on. His legs were like matchsticks, it was so funny. His brother put him on his shoulders and then put their dad's big coat on.

At that time there wasn't much birth control available – if there was I wasn't getting it. I tried again but, even after all I had been through, the doctor still wouldn't sterilise me. By chance one day, the doctor had been visiting my next-door neighbour who was pregnant and had difficulties. He knocked my door and just walked in saying

'Come on upstairs, get a bowl of hot water! I can do your postnatal examination and then I can write you out a prescription for the pill.'

I felt so embarrassed but he was in a rush and wanted to get on with it. I didn't have any hot water just cold so that had to do. He carried on and examined me and I went on the pill after that.

I had a total of 10 pregnancies, three miscarriages and seven children and I just couldn't cope with any more. We only had a small house. I was going to work every day scrubbing floors then coming home to more work. Space was limited in the house and there was no washing machine; I had to boil all the water up. That is exactly how it was, never-ending. My nappies were grey; they were the old Terry nappies made of squares of towelling. It was very hard work boiling them and getting them dry. The only toilet was outside with no light. Every time one of the children went outside to the toilet in the dark they called out

'Mum, can you come and get me, it's dark?'

Ray never shared the workload with me. The only time he helped was when I was rock bottom and then he cooked the meals but that was all.

One day I saw a big car pull up outside of our house. The window was wound down and a man was holding a big movie camera facing our house. The man knocked the front door and when I opened it another man was standing there holding a packet of Daz washing powder. He said

'Have you got a packet of Daz in the house love?'

'No, I am sorry but I haven't. I have got a packet of Tide,' I replied.

There was a promotion on at the time advertised on the television. If you could produce a packet of Daz you would instantly win some money. My family could have been featured on a television advertisement. I was so disappointed, who would have believed that they would knock on my door? I just wish now that I had had the courage to say I had a family of six kids and could have done with the prize-money. I should have been quicker and got the kids to come and stand beside me. The man may have felt sorry for me and decided that we really did need the money.

Even a packet of Daz would have been useful at the time and he could have given me a packet of Daz and taken a photo. My big family of kids would have been a good picture to feature on one of their adverts. We would have received £10 for producing a packet of Daz. Ten pounds was a lot of money to us in those days and would have meant we could buy food. I didn't even have a halfpenny in my pocket when the man called.

17

Family matters

Ray was a believer in psychic matters. My psychic powers are much stronger now than they were when I was younger. I think I had too much responsibility then so it couldn't have worked as well for me. I have believed in the spirit world since I was a young child. We had our first child christened in a spiritualist church. Ray didn't object to that, he was all for it. You either believe in it or you don't. Ray believed in spirits and ghosts too.

Ray visited his brother, Les, who lived near us. Les was big and strong just like Ray was. He did all the acetylene burning for Seymour's the iron merchants. If a boat needed lifting Les was the only man who could do it. Or if the front of a car needed lifting, Les would do it. They both had a reputation for being strong. So when Ray became ill his heart problem did not show and so his death was a great shock to everyone.

Les was married to Norah who was a funny woman to talk to. She could have been no more than four foot high and Les was very tall. They lived at the end of Warren Avenue, near St James's Hospital in a wooden hut. Several of the wooden huts were occupied then and eventually people were re-housed and the huts were demolished. Les had a photo of me leaning against a wooden wall when I was a young lass of 18. He used to say

'That's my girlfriend and Ray was lucky.'

One evening he had been watching the 'Bootsie & Snudge' programme on the television and when it had finished he said to Norah

'I have got chronic indigestion, will you get me a glass of water and a Beecham's Powder please?'

Les drank down the mixture and it gurgled in his throat. Norah said after that he went funny. She shook him saying

'Les, Les, what's the matter?'

Norah got into a panic and didn't know what to do. She ran along the road and knocked on someone's door and asked them to come and have a look at her husband because something was wrong with him. When they got back Les was dead.

Les died from a genetic heart complaint. Ray and Les's mum had 17 children. Their parents owned a greengrocer's business and the old man broke it all up because the old girl kept on giving people credit. The old man said

'There's no money in the till because you keep giving credit. I will show you what credit is!'

So with that he broke the shop and the cart up.

Both Ray and Les died of the same genetic heart problem. My boys have to be careful but I always tell them

'Don't get worried because you have got a good bit of me in you.'

They know I am strong. They say

'Mum, we have seen you fight our dad.'

I knew I would always get a real hard kick after hitting back at Ray but I said to him

'If you degrade me you degrade my kids and I will thump you.'

I did have that courage. In later years I always stood up to him. I usually paid dearly for it afterwards though. It was an awful marriage.

If Ray was still alive he would have thrown all of the kids out. He threw Yvonne out once because she came in three minutes later than the deadline he had set for her. In those days we had to rely on buses to travel around and if the bus was late there was nothing we could do about it. She came in three minutes late and he clipped her around the face, opened the front door and said

'Get out!'

I said to him

'That is my daughter you are throwing out; you can throw me out too!'

So I walked out with her.

We were walking along Cranleigh Road away from the house and Yvonne said

'Mum, what are we going to do?'

'Don't worry; we won't even get around the corner. He won't let me go, I am too bloody useful,' I said.

Sure enough, I was right. We had not even reached the top of the road when Ray came running along. He had no shoes on and he ran like a thunderbolt down the road. We waited for the explosion! He shouted to me

'Get in you cow, you bitch, get home!'

He swore at me and he was so angry that I had dared to defy him in that way. So Yvonne and I went back home.

One Easter Sunday evening Ray took me to bingo. We couldn't sit next to each other because it was a packed house. Ray had never been to bingo before and after a while he shouted out 'house' and held his card up. I thought he had probably got it wrong as he had never played the game before. A woman came and checked his card and it was correct. She went away and then came back with a brown envelope which was bulging with used notes. We couldn't believe it. When we got home the kids all scattered back to bed because they shouldn't have been up.

Ray opened the envelope and threw the money up in the air – I had never seen him so happy. He was shouting out

'Alright, who wants some money? Come on down, come downstairs.'

All the kids came tumbling down the stairs and we were all laughing at Ray throwing all this money around. It was a lovely, happy time and we felt like millionaires. It was over £300, which at that time was a lot of money.

Ray took everything so seriously and he only had a sense of humour when he was with his friends. He was always the boss. If one of us started laughing about something he wanted to shut us up. One time we were going to visit Yvonne who was living in Bristol then. This was our first car and we all settled down for the journey. The atmosphere was happy. The kids had a black Labrador dog which had been a stray and we decided to keep him in the family. The kids had to plead with their dad to take the dog with us to Yvonne's house.

The dog was called Prince but we all called him Prinny. We took Prinny with us but it was quite a long journey from Portsmouth to Bristol. I was sitting in the back with the kids and the dog, trying to keep the dog calm and quiet.

When we got three quarters of the way to Bristol, Prinny started whining. Ray said

'Shut that bloody dog up will you!'

The kids and I were saying Shhh to the dog and holding his mouth closed. Eventually Prinny whined so much that Ray pulled the car over to the side of the road, flung open the door and jumped out of the car. He said

'Get that dog out of there, get him out!'

Prinny was only too glad to get out of the car and Ray told us all to get back into the car. Graham knew what Ray was going to do. He was going to drive off and leave the dog behind.

I know this is not a funny story but this is just how it happened. Graham got on his hands and knees on the ground and was pleading with his dad saying

'Please don't leave the dog behind, please don't leave him here.'

In the end Ray relented and allowed the dog back into the car again. You couldn't argue with Ray and it always upset the kids if there was an argument. He was a very unrelenting person, what he said went – he was the master of all. Whatever I said to him didn't make any difference.

Another time we decided to go camping to Sandy Balls Holiday Village, in the New Forest. Ray borrowed an ex-army tent from the father of one of Yvonne's friends. We parked on the edge of the grass away from everyone else. Ray was having difficulty putting the tent up and it looked so funny that we started giggling. I said to the kids

'Don't let your dad see you laughing.'

Anyway Ray came out covered in sweat and said

'I don't know how to handle this tent.'

Of course he caught us all laughing and his face darkened as he shouted

'If you don't stop laughing we are going home right now, this minute!'

He said it with real vengeance; he was so angry and embarrassed because he couldn't put the tent up.

A man opposite had been watching us and he came over to us and said

'Excuse me, I hope you don't mind me telling you, but you have got the tent the wrong way round.'

My imagination ran riot then and I started laughing again. I could imagine us in the middle of the night being smothered with the tent with us all pinned down beneath it. We stifled our giggling and the man very kindly put the tent up for us and it looked good.

We had borrowed two inflatable beds and other camping equipment from Yvonne's friend as well. It was cold at night and damp and rabbits were running all around the tent outside. Of course I had the dud air mattress which would only inflate at one end. The lower half of me was lying on the ground. I couldn't get back to sleep lying like that with my top half sitting up and when I looked around me everyone was fast asleep. Ray was covered over and snoring his head off and I was just sitting there wide awake.

That was the first and last time I ever went camping. It was so uncomfortable. We were trying to handle a fire and cook burnt porridge and beans. Then it started raining and everything got soaked and muddy. I hated it, I really hated it. There was entertainment in the evening and lots of other campers all around us. Although we didn't have much money we ended up staying for about five days and overall we did enjoy it. It certainly gave us all something to laugh about for years.

Some years later my daughter Diane and I made different types of clothing for a shop called Diane Ashman's. It was at the end of Elm Grove in Southsea. We were voted second best shop in Portsmouth. That is a real tribute when you are sewing with rags! You name it, we made it. We made 1920s dresses out of sheets with antique lace trimming and we made men's gangster-type suits to sell in the shop. We bought naval sheets which we cut up and had to boil first. We made patterns, I could draw and I knew how to make a pattern. I could see instinctively what was needed.

The shop owner asked me if I would like to buy the shop for £7,000 but it would have been £10,000 if I had got a bank loan. I dearly wanted to buy it. My daughter and I worked together and we used to laugh so much we were in tears. We loved those days and that is why we are so close now.

18

Ray's progress

My husband was a big drinker and he always had to be one of the lads in the pub. His best friend was a man called John Morris and he owned a Spar grocery shop. They both came from big families so they had a lot in common and they drank in the pub together. Other friends joined them and they stood at the bar, laughing and joking. My husband drank his week's wages and the children and I were living on a pittance and we often went hungry. It was no good me asking him for more money because he drank it and so there wasn't any. It was a waste of time.

Ray started becoming ill with his heart. He was a big man and was always so fit but he had a genetic heart problem. He didn't know that though until much later. Ray drank and he smoked cigarettes. He also ate meat but the rest of us couldn't eat meat because we couldn't afford it.

I was at work one day cleaning the bar in the Shearer Arms pub and later that night Ray became sick. He was sick the next morning and he had some form of a seizure as well. He was so ill I thought he was going to turn himself inside out with all the retching and vomiting. It was awful. After I had got the kids ready and off to school I made a doctor's appointment for him.

We waited in the doctor's surgery; it was very quiet and I had an uneasy feeling. The doctor examined Ray and listened to his chest and back several times. We had known Doctor Eddings for a long time; he had seen me through some of my pregnancies. I asked if it was Ray's stomach that was the problem. He replied that it wasn't his stomach but his 'ticker', his heart.

After the examination I looked up at Ray buttoning his shirt and he looked as though he could have cried. He was relieved that his pain had finally been acknowledged but he was frightened about what could be wrong with him and didn't like to admit how bad it was. Dr Eddings prescribed nitroglycerin tablets, one to be placed under the tongue when he felt pain. Apparently Ray had angina. We had never heard of angina before.

We went back home and I went on to work. The girls came in to the shop later in the day and I asked

'How's your dad?'

They said he was alright and was asleep in the armchair. I asked if he had been taking his tablets. They said

'Yes, he keeps on taking them.'

'What do you mean he keeps on taking them? He is only supposed to take one every time he has a pain.'

I didn't like the sound of that.

After work I walked home laden with shopping. I arrived indoors and looked at the bottle of pills and there were only a few left! The tablets dissolved under the tongue and stopped the pain in the heart. I said

'How many pills have you taken? You are only supposed to take one when you have a pain.'

'That's how many pains I have had,' he said.

I called the doctor early the next morning before I went to work. I was working at Olivers shoe shop by then. I had to come home from town in my lunch hour, see the doctor and rush back to the bus and on to work. The doctor said he would have to get a specialist in to see Ray.

The specialist duly came and examined Ray. He wanted him to go into hospital because he had some pressure at the back of his neck. I had the feeling that the doctor was making some sort of an excuse just to get Ray into hospital. Ray always had a fear of going into hospital because he thought that if he went in he would never come out again.

The next morning an ambulance arrived to take Ray to hospital but he wouldn't go in. For three days an ambulance turned up for him and each time he refused to go. The driver was furious and slammed the ambulance door shut. I talked to Ray about it, saying that a doctor and a specialist thought he should be in hospital. He just said

'It's up to me whether I want to go in or not!'

At that time Ray managed to work his illness off and he returned to normal, although it took a good six months for him to fully recover. During that time he was not working and was signing on the dole. After that, every time I saw the doctor myself, he asked how Ray was. I told him that he was alright now and had eventually gone back to work. The doctor just kept saying 'He was very lucky there.'

Some weeks after that Ray came in and told me that he had a job interview that afternoon at Portsmouth dockyard.

'The dockyard!' I said.

'You said you were going to run all the dockies on their bikes over with your car because there are so many of them. Now you are telling me that you are going to work in the dockyard.'

He went to the interview and got the job as a 'slinger'. He was so big and strong and the men loved him because he was the 'big wig'. They were in awe of his muscles.

Ray was enjoying the job in the dockyard and decided to keep it. He was a 'slinger', handling the big chains and loading cargo onto ships. It was the last thing he should have been doing really but we didn't know that then. It is ironic but he loved that job. He came and picked me up from work; I was working in Ravel's shoe shop by that time. One day he told me that he had felt quite funny at work with chronic indigestion. He just didn't know what to do with himself. I asked him why he hadn't gone to the medical room. He said

'Look at me. A big giant of a man like me and smaller men

working with me, what are they going to say "What a wimp, going to the medical room!"'

'What did you do then?' I asked. He said he went and hid himself until it had eased off a bit. It was like that in those days so he didn't go to the sick bay.

Ray had been working at the dockyard for about six months and he met me from work at the back of the Ravel's shoe shop in Commercial Road. He parked the car there and waited for me. It was hard work but I was top saleswoman there. I got an extra £1 for that accolade. I was very good at my job; I could serve four people at the same time.

That evening we had dinner and sat down afterwards. Later on Ray took some tablets for his indigestion and went up to bed early because he felt so tired. Ray came back downstairs again and said that it was so uncomfortable and painful lying down that he had to sit back up again. Eventually he thought he might just as well get up. At around 11 o'clock Ray said he would drive to the Royal Hospital and see a doctor. This type of behaviour was alien to Ray so he must have felt really unwell. He asked me to go with him and I said

'Are you sure? Supposing there is nothing wrong with you and they send you back home again saying it was just indigestion? You will feel a right fool.'

He was always a big macho man and this was so unlike him. He couldn't drive in that state so we walked to the hospital.

Inside the casualty department there was not a soul in sight. We looked along corridors and into rooms but there was no one about. It was if they had all gone home but the lights were left on. After a little while sitting there Ray said

'Come on I think we will go back home, I feel a little brighter now.'

He had taken more Rennies indigestion tablets by then and so we returned home.

A few days later he went to see Dr. Eddings who gave him some tablets. Ray asked the doctor to give him a sick note for the couple of days he had been off work. The doctor looked up and said

'I will tell you when you can go back to work!'

It all felt so eerie and unreal. Everything seemed to be working opposite to the way it should be. Before that Ray would have said 'So what, I have had some days off, if work doesn't like it I will walk out.' He always said that but this time he wanted a proper medical certificate to say that he was ill – and this time he was allowed to stay at home.

Ray was still feeling unwell the next day and I said to him

'You lay down on the settee, the kids are out to play so it is nice and quiet. You can lie down and go to sleep and I will sit with you and watch the television.'

He started laughing and I said

'What are you laughing at?'

'I am laughing at you fussing over me,' he said.

Well, he was ill after all and he was not used to being fussed over. He felt cold so I got him a blanket and a pillow. He couldn't stop grinning and thought it was very funny. He eventually drifted off to sleep.

After a while Ray woke and sat up and asked me to get him a bucket because he felt sick. I got a bucket and he was violently sick. He was leaning over the bucket with his horn-rimmed glasses on. Sheree and I were looking at him and I nudged her and said

'He is crying.'

His glasses were wet. I felt so sorry for him then. I put my arm around him and he was red hot. I told Sheree something was wrong. I said I was going over to a neighbour, Mrs Smith's house, to ask to use the phone to call the doctor. Everyone knew Ray was a layabout and was always in the pub. So when I asked Mrs Smith if I could use her phone because Ray was ill, she looked at me with disbelief and said

'Oh, he's ill again is he?'

She did let me use the phone to call the doctor thankfully.

The doctor visited us straight away; it was about 7 o'clock in the evening by then. Ray was in an awful state and the doctor examined him, felt his ankles, took his pulse, sounded his chest and said

'I am calling an ambulance; you will have to go straight to hospital.'

I repeated to him that he had to go into hospital and he couldn't talk, he just nodded his head.

The ambulance men came and carried him in because he had said he wouldn't go in unless he was carried in! I went with him to hospital. I was crying so much and I knew that it was very serious and that something was really wrong with Ray. I seemed to instinctively know what the outcome was going to be. I often had insight like that and I seemed to always be right when I had it.

Ray was put into an emergency room because he was having a heart attack. I was sobbing my heart out and a young woman came and sat with me. I have always had nice people come to me in bad situations. She put her arm around me and said

'Don't worry, everything will be alright.' Everyone went into the ward to visit and when she came out she sat beside me again.

'Look, I don't know how to tell you this but I have seen your husband and he is all wired up in there. I thought I would just let you know to pre-warn you.'

'Thank you, you have been so kind,' I replied.

I always think that God or a spirit has looked after me and sent somebody nice to me. I went in and it was true, Ray was all wired up. He couldn't speak to me but I held his hand. I was facing the wall and the heart monitor was on the ward sister's desk. I sat there and after a while they told me that I had to leave.

I visited him the next day and he seemed a bit brighter but was still wired up to the heart monitor.

The following day something had changed. He was in a real deep sleep and didn't know I was there. I looked at the activity on the heart monitor and I didn't like the look of it. I was sitting facing the window and holding his hand. I didn't wake him up but he knew I was there and apparently it was distressing him. He must have been half-conscious but it was stressing him and that is what I could see on the monitor. The doctor came in and checked the monitor. He said

'I am sorry; you will have to go home because you being here is distressing your husband.'

It made me cry. I was just sitting there with him, I couldn't believe it. As much I may have hated Ray, I still had some love for him. We love people sometimes more than we realise and it is at times like that we feel it.

That evening was a cold, crisp night with frost on the ground glistening in the moonlight. The hospital wasn't far from where we lived and as I was walking home over St. Mary's bridge I had a feeling that Ray would not be coming home. I cried all the way home. By the time I arrived home I was thinking that maybe he would come home after all. When all the kids asked about him I told them he wasn't very well but that he was managing and was on good medication.

 ❧

I went to work the next day believing that Ray was going to get better. My neighbour, Mrs Smith's son, Ian, came into the shoe shop while I was at work and told me he had been sent by the hospital to come and get me. Ray had had a turn for the worse and I was to go to the hospital immediately. Ian drove me to the hospital straight away.

When we arrived at the hospital Ray had been moved into another unit. He had suffered another big heart attack and the doctor had to inject straight into his heart. Again he couldn't talk. The doctor told me this was very serious as it was the second big attack and the heart could only take so much. Ray was a man who made his own decisions and he would never be any different. No one could tell him or warn him about anything; once he had made up his mind about something that was it. It was my birthday soon and Ray had managed to get a card for me and signed it. He thought he was coming home for Christmas and would be let out of hospital a day or two before if he was good. I put the card in my handbag and thought oh well, that's another birthday gone.

Ray was moved onto a ward. The two friends he had made in the other ward were moved into the new ward with him. This ward was for the more serious cases and was nearer to the medical team desk.

Ray was still in hospital on Christmas Day. I sent all the kids in to see him with Christmas presents and they sat around his bed. I stayed home to prepare and cook the Christmas dinner and told the kids to tell him that we would all visit him in the afternoon after we had eaten dinner together. We ate our Christmas dinner and then later we all went back to the hospital and had a sing-song around the bed. We tried to make it nice and friendly for the other two men in there as well. Ray's face looked as white as the pillow. He looked awful.

Later, when we arrived home, I said to the kids

'Come on kids we are going to have a Christmas day if it's the last thing we do.'

We started to get the food and drink organised when there was a knock at the front door. There were two lads standing there so I asked them in. One of them was Harry Fenton (from Harry Fenton's menswear shop) and his mate. Harry was going out with Marian at the time. I invited them in and wished them a merry Christmas. My front door was always open to people. I said

'Come on let us all have our own Christmas now. Come on Marian get them a drink.'

Harry said

'Excuse me Mrs Jones but the police were following us down the road.'

'You have been speeding, haven't you?' I said.

'No, we haven't been speeding,' said Harry.

He had real fuzzy black hair. I said

'Yes, you have; you are having me on aren't you? Why would the police be in our road?'

I was so oblivious of what was happening. Then a policeman knocked on the front door. I was indignant by this time because I was thinking 'Leave the lads alone, it's Christmas Day.' He said

'Mrs Jones, have you just come back from the hospital?'

'Yes,' I said.

It didn't dawn on me that there was anything wrong. I just didn't have a clue! I still thought Ray was going to get better because he was so strong. I had left him asleep at the hospital and his last words to me were 'Get me some mixers to go with the whiskey from John Morris at the Spar shop please.'

The hospital had phoned the police and asked them to escort me back there. I left the kids and told them to enjoy themselves as I was going back to the hospital. Marian insisted on coming to the hospital with me. On the way to the hospital I was saying to the policeman 'It must be awful working on Christmas Day. Thank you for taking us to the hospital.' Keith went to tell John Morris what was happening. John knew something wasn't right with Ray. He immediately left his family and guests and drove to the hospital. Keith went upstairs and shut himself in his bedroom. It was a very sombre time in the house because even though their dad had not been very nice to them they still loved him.

As we walked up the stairs in the hospital it was deathly quiet all along the corridors and right into the ward. I knew then that something had happened. The ward sister met us, walked us into her office and offered us a cup of tea. Marian and I sat there with a cup of tea; a very tall well-built doctor with ginger hair came in, sat down and pulled his chair up close to mine. Our knees were almost touching. He said

'We did everything we could, we had the whole team working around him but he had already gone.'

As soon as I had left the hospital Ray had died. He was 42 years old!

That was the third heart attack he had, besides being ill before and I just couldn't believe it. I couldn't take the news in, I felt totally numb. The doctor said

'Would you like to see him?'

'Yes, I would. I won't believe it until I have seen him with my own eyes.'

There he was; he looked pale but he just looked as if he was asleep. I said

'I am so sorry Ray.'

Tears were rolling down my cheeks. John Morris came in and stood beside me and he was sobbing. He was heartbroken. I had never seen a man cry like that before. It was a very bleak and devastating time.

The other two men in the ward had witnessed Ray's heart attack; I felt so sorry for them. I gave one of the men my cigarette lighter and said he could keep it. Later on he came to see me and gave me the lighter back. He said

'The staff didn't do very much; they were sitting in there enjoying themselves.'

He had to push the button and he told them

'Get your asses out here there is a man dying.'

'That is wrong!'

John came into the hospital saying

'I knew it; I knew there was something wrong with Ray. I left all my family at home and I have come to see my mate.'

I didn't know John was coming to the hospital and I didn't know my son Keith had gone to tell him about Ray. Yvonne had bought a large bottle of whiskey and Ray had asked Keith to go to the Spar shop and buy some mixers so they could have a Christmas drink. Ray wanted to give all the team a drink too as well as the big box of chocolates we had bought for them. The kids had all bought him lovely presents in spite of his behaviour with them, especially the lads.

Some time later John drove us home. When we got in Marian and Diane were crying. Diane was nine years old and she said

'Why did daddy have to die?'

'Well darling, it is Jesus's birthday today and Jesus had sent daddy an invitation to go to his party and so he has gone.' I was in such shock it was the only thing I could think of to say. Diane said

'Yes, but I wanted him here as well.'

Ray was a big part of all our lives; we had been married for 22 years and we had been through a lot together. I suddenly realised that I was alone with a family of kids and they were my responsibility.

I had to pick up the pieces and carry on. I thought

'I am the boss.'

It was the first time in my life that I was in charge completely.

Ray is now in spirit waiting for me to die and he will come to meet me when it is my time. How strange is that? He was down for the birth of my latest great-grandson and he was there before the birth. His presence was very evident. He made all the lights flick on and off in celebration as the birth happened. The birth was a difficult one because the baby weighed eleven pounds; he was enormous. All Ray's family were tall and were a beautiful family. Ray was destined to be in my life. I feel that he will be in another lifetime with me and I hope he will have realised his mistakes in this life and be playing a better role.

19

Spiritual awakening

Ray died on Christmas day, 25th December 1973. It was a shocking and devastating blow to all the family. We had to get on with our lives the best way we could. Yvonne, our eldest child, was aged 21 and Diane, the youngest, was nine years old.

It was the start of a new year and I had to go back to my job – I didn't want to but knew I had to in order to keep my family together. I was a single parent and the main bread-winner now. I carried on working as much as I could to pay the rent, food and clothing and the older children were contributing towards the household by then.

Life went on and later in 1974 my 14 year-old daughter, Sheree, had booked to see Len Burden for a psychic reading. She was supposed to be going with her friend but at the last minute her friend could not go. Sheree knew that I was interested in spiritual matters and so she talked me into going to see Len with her.

Len Burden was a well-known Portsmouth medium and he was aged around 30 at that time. He had dark hair and had a tanned complexion. My daughter was a little nervous beforehand and she asked me to go in and see Len first. I walked into a semi-dark room; there was a picture of the last supper on an altar at the end of the room. I sat there facing Len and I didn't know quite what to expect. He told me I had three people in spirit there with me. Two were men and I presumed one was my dad and I think the other one might have been my granddad. The other was a lady who I at first thought was my mum but it couldn't have been my mum because I found out after that she was still alive. I remember Len talking and I was listening and then an overwhelming feeling came over me, just like a cosy cloak had been wrapped all around me. I felt very comfortable and really at ease. Apparently, I was told later, I had gone into a trance.

I remember that when I came out of the trance Len put his dark-rimmed glasses on and he turned around and looked at me. He lifted his glasses and looked at me again. I couldn't understand why he was looking at me like that. At the end of the session he said to me

'My dear the Sagittarian sign is glowing right over your head, it is absolutely glowing and it looks beautiful. What birth sign are you?'

'I am Sagittarian,' I replied. He told me that as I got older my life would be a lot happier. That was just over 40 years ago now.

Sheree went in to see him next. He said to her (and he didn't know I was her mother)

'That is an incredible lady who has just passed you. She has just transfigured into three different people and one of them was my own mother. I have never had that happen to me before. It was amazing.'

Afterwards my daughter told Len that I was her mother. He said 'Well, my dear, you won't appreciate her, not for a long time.'

I never thought that Sheree and I would be sitting here together as we are now because we were apart for 20 years. She blamed me for letting her dad die when he was so young. She went to live and work in London for several years and travelled to Italy, the Himalayas, India – you name it and she has done it. She just wanted to travel and see the world.

Len Burden was meant to come into my life and it is funny, that what people do is they will show themselves one way or another. I had no idea that years later I would play a part in Len's life also.

After Ray died I went to a local psychic medium for a reading. Here is an extract of part of the reading:

I have a woman here, she was an arty, farty sort of person. She was an artist and was musical and she couldn't cope with life. She is saying sorry to you for what she did to you. You had to be the woman of the house before you were old enough to know anything. She is saying: 'Sorry, I could not cope with the world.' She was a lady, she had nice hands and was very pretty. 'Please forgive me' she is saying. She is giving you a bouquet of yellow flowers for forgiveness. She is with you quite a lot.

I have someone with a bad chest. You get weary and depressed and you think about what life should have been like or what could have been better. There's a man standing at the back of you. He is with you quite a lot and it is your late husband. He died young. He's saying he knows he did things wrong but he was one of the lads. He didn't want to stop and he didn't want to grow up. He was a Peter Pan; he thought he had no responsibilities and that you could deal with it all. He is not asking forgiveness though. He is here with you now and he's saying it was his loss and that he 'did his bit' as well by giving you all those children and you have had them around you but he hasn't.

Who bought you a watch? Well, your first husband is standing behind you with a red rose and he is saying he always loved you and he regretted such a lot and knew he was going to go and fought quite hard to stay as well. It was a sudden death. He knew that he was going to have this end but he pushed and pushed his health. It was mostly his own fault. There was money taken and he says that's one of his regrets as well. He spent money on his selfish self that should have been put into the family and he regrets it. You weren't always unhappy with your first husband. You loved him so much and he always returned the love but he didn't always return the partnership or look after the children. He was a bit of a chancer and he's saying he took one last gamble and lost it. It was his heart; it was unexpected and a shock. I can see you crying and you have always worked hard and you have done this for your children. You have always worked hard with your hands and the spirits are saying you didn't just want to survive, you wanted more than that for your children.

I have your brother now. You are quite alike and he is artistic as well. There were quite a lot of things you could have done together but you never got the chance. You were too lonely and although you have always been strong there were lots of tears.

I can see a big place with lots of children (the remand homes) and there was a big wall around it and you felt like climbing it and running *away. They were unhappy days for you. You felt grief and abandonment. You went through a mourning period as if someone had died. You were worried and anxious and did you stop speaking? I feel that was terrible for you. There was also someone there who you were terrified of. Someone who was picking on people and bullying them and taking away their dignity. It was an older person and that is how they got their kicks. This person came to a sad end. Whoever it was you may be pleased to know it was a man and he came to a sad and lonely end and he knew exactly what he had done.*

You had a job to learn because you were sad but you wanted to learn because you enjoyed it but it was knocked out of you. You were planning to prove to everyone that when you got out you would show them all. Were you close to someone there, a special friend and they made a bond with you. They want to be remembered to you. You were very pretty, beautiful. You got your confidence up and blossomed and you worked in an engineering factory and there was a bond with someone who you made friends with there. She used to wear her hair up in a scarf and she wasn't very pretty. She is saying you had laughs together.

A broken engagement ring that was put on and then taken straight back off again – his mother was involved. Did he go very thin? There were things said that you never forgot. He was in a turmoil, frustration.

You have got worries about the health of Andy. There is sometimes aggression with him which is unusual for him. It's his illness that does this. I also feel that he hallucinates or sees things sometimes. It is his medication, it frightens him I feel. He is missing you in some way, he misses the old days when you were happier. There will come a time when you will need help with him although you are so independent. Ask spirit to help. Also you must get help from others too. Spirit will help you with your worries. He won't get an awful lot worse for a while. You must talk to the doctor. You are a sunny person who loves the sun and you are always busy. You are to come to terms with your childhood and your brother will help you but you are to look to the future and enjoy what you can, be at peace. You will always be busy and happy. You will be painting pictures. Spirit helps you paint.

Christmas is a hard time for you and your first husband is saying he couldn't have gone on a better day when everyone was enjoying themselves. He will be there when you need help.

Charlie, your granddad, is saying that your dad could have done more and that he should have put his foot down more in his marriage. Charlie was a strong character and your father wasn't. Charlie loved him though and he was angry with him for committing suicide. It wasn't just your mother who caused it there were other things involved too. I've got a man's voice here. A soft-spoken man, very gentle. He couldn't cope with life either and there were certain things that happened in his past life that nobody knew about though and this all contributed to it. He found peace and happiness on the other side and he regrets doing it. He knew as soon as he did it that he shouldn't have done it. He should have stayed for you and your brother. You will see him again though and you will see him as you remember him. He comes to you with a lot of love and one red rose and he's saying to me that you speak to him and tell him your problems. He's always there for you, so always talk to him.

20

Inspired images

I have drawn and painted pictures all of my life and many years ago I belonged to a local art group. Before Ray died he allowed me to go out on a Wednesday evening for about two hours. Una was my neighbour and she accompanied me to the art class. Her husband sang in a local pub and they had two children: a son and daughter. There was an adult education centre near Mile End where a Mr Palmer taught art. I always wanted to learn how to paint with oils. I could use water colour paint but I had never touched oil and pastels. My talent for drawing came from being on my own a lot as a child, having a piece of paper and a pencil and just seeing things I wanted to draw. I didn't have any money to buy materials and so I was lucky to be able to paint at all.

But I did paint and as fast as I finished a painting, it was gone; people bought them from me or I gave them away. I painted all the old masters. All the paintings found good homes. At one time I had to nail down one of my paintings to the floor to cover a hole in the floorboards in the house. You would never believe that I was a mum with all those kids and with so little money to create paintings with.

Una and I enjoyed the classes and we entered our work in exhibitions. One week Una was painting some beautiful apple blossom and as she was trying to mix up some paint, I looked at the painting and I started laughing, I just couldn't help it. She had worked so hard to get that colour and it just didn't look at all right. We both ended up in a fit of the giggles.

I painted a lady on a swing surrounded by woods and trees. She had a 17th century dress on and her slippers were just floating as the swing went higher. Her lover was hiding in the bushes but it was her husband who was pushing the swing!

I loved going to those art classes because I had freedom, even though it was only for a couple of hours. I produced quite a few paintings and got nominated by readers of our local newspaper for first and second prizes. My first painting was on show at the NAAFI club in Southampton.

My son Graham's arm had swollen up and it was very red. I didn't like the look of it so I took him to the Accident and Emergency Department at The Royal Hospital in Portsmouth. (The Royal Hospital closed in 1979.) We saw Dr. Eddings, who was our family doctor and happened to be on duty at the time. I explained that there was something wrong with Graham's arm. Dr. Eddings said he couldn't stop and that there was another doctor on duty who would look at Graham's arm. As he walked away he said 'Oh, congratulations, your painting was voted first prize by the public at the NAAFI.' We didn't buy the local paper *The News* so I hadn't seen the article. It was just a tiny column in the newspaper.

The view was of Lake Menteith in Scotland with the moon shining on the water. There was an island in the middle with a large tree and a person standing on the bank. A small boat was floating on the water with two figures in it. I was intrigued by Lake Menteith because Scottish chieftains had been buried on the island. Apparently the public voted my painting first out of 90 or so contributors. I was very thrilled because I never think my paintings are good enough.

Some time later I went to an art class in Havant run by a Mr Nicholski. He was an artist in his own right and he was Russian. He painted HMS Victory which was enlarged and printed on large posters. He did a demonstration at The Tricorn in Portsmouth of a portrait in oils. I went to his classes but all I did was paint flowers and not one portrait. I learnt a lot from him in the short time that I went there but it was some miles away from my home and it was usually a rush for me to get to the class. I always had to fit things into such a short time. I did enjoy my time there and it was a very useful experience learning from a professional.

I did a lot of painting at home and one day a man knocked on my door. He was an antique dealer and he had seen some of my paintings. He later sold some of them and in fact he took and sold everything I gave him. The very first picture he took was by the French artist Louise-Elisabeth Vigee-Lebrun. I loved that painting, it was very flamboyant and I painted it twice. It was displayed on an easel in his shop window. A lady went in and bought the painting and asked for it to be packed carefully because it was going all the way to Australia. That was the very first painting he had from me. He later had to give up the shop because he went bankrupt so that little enterprise stopped.

Another venture was through a friend of mine who bought second-hand crockery from the mills in the north of England. He brought the crockery to me and I hand painted it. It was difficult to do repeat artwork on crockery but I did it and then I baked it in the oven as I didn't have a kiln. Everything I have attempted was short-lived and wasn't meant to be, sadly. This pattern repeated right throughout my life even right up to the artwork I am doing now.

A rare piece of luck actually came my way one time. My daughter, Di, and her family had gone away on holiday and I was missing them and feeling lonely. As usual I had no money at all so I thought I would go for a walk for something to do. A family birthday was coming up so I went into town to just look for a gift; I thought I would return and buy it when I did have some money. I walked into Portsmouth without a halfpenny in my pocket when it began to rain. People were rushing around everywhere and as I was walking I was observing their faces and clothing and wondering what jobs they had and what they were doing in their daily lives. I carried on walking, past the back of the railway station goods yard, near to the Guildhall and the taxi rank. A little further on I looked on the ground and I could see a piece of coloured, dirty creased paper.

It was still pouring with rain and the paper was stuck to the ground. I couldn't make out what it was and I was so intrigued that I stooped down and picked it up. I held it up and I could see the number 50 on it. I turned it over and looked at it again; then I could make out the shape of a crown. I turned it over and through the dirt I could just make out the words 'Fifty Pounds'. I had never seen a £50 note before so I read it again and again and I thought 'No, it can't be.' I didn't believe that it could be a real £50 note, it must be a fake.

I looked at it over and over several times because it was difficult for me to convince myself that I was holding an authentic £50 note. People had walked all over it and I just couldn't believe my luck! The only explanation I could think of was that a taxi driver had been stuffing money into his wallet and one note had dropped out and blown away and he probably hadn't even noticed it. It had obviously been on the ground for a long time.

Oh my God, I couldn't believe my luck! I went straight into Sainsbury's and spent nearly three-quarters of it on food to stock up my empty kitchen cupboards at home. I had literally been at rock bottom and was feeling so down-hearted and lonely before I found it. The feeling of elation and relief just flooded through me.

I have received painting commissions over the years from many people. There was a picture-framing and art shop near to where I live. The owner visited my home and saw my work on display but he wasn't too keen at first because he felt that my subjects were mostly spiritual. He wanted to sell some works from his shop and he asked me to paint a picture from a magazine. His idea was that he would display the picture in his shop and I was to get a share of the royalties from any sale or prints/copies made. I love painting pictures of women. The picture he wanted painting was of Mother Gaia. I found the original picture rather dull so of course I added my own interpretation to it. I added extra colour and embellishments to make it more vibrant. I called it *Gaia's Abundance*.

21

Art and Andy

After Ray died I started picking up the pieces and getting on with life. After quite some time I returned to my previous art class again. One day my friend, Una, said to me

'My old man is going to the pub tonight to do his singing. I told him I was going to the art class but how about you and I go to the Mecca instead?'

I said alright I would go but I didn't really fancy going to the Mecca. Then I thought it would be something different and she had an opportunity to go, so off we went. The Mecca was our local dancing club. Una was a good friend of mine and she was good fun to be with; we often had a giggle together. We had quite a nice time at the Mecca that night and we danced together. At the end Una said we should do the same again sometime.

After about our third time of going to the Mecca, we had bought ourselves a drink and were sitting at a table on the edge of the dance floor busily talking. Two fellows came and asked us for a dance, so we got up, left our drinks and started dancing. We had three dances with these two men. I went back to the table but our drinks had gone – and so had Una! There was no sign of her on the dance floor. The man I had been dancing with asked if I would like a drink. I said 'Yes please.' I thought I might as well because I didn't know where Una had gone and I decided to sit down and wait for her. We took our drinks upstairs and sat looking over the dance floor. He spoke in a Birmingham (Brummie) accent and all he could talk about was football, football, football – it was awful! I said goodbye to him and he said he would see me again in the Mecca. I wasn't bothered at all.

Una and I went to the Mecca again several more times and how many times was I picked up there? The men used to say

'Where have you been all my life?'

They were all ages, older and younger than I was. I danced with most of the men who asked me because I loved to dance. There was one fellow who every time he saw me made a beeline for me and we had three dances together. He danced very well and was a really good lead dancer. He was quite a big man but he didn't speak to me at all. We had exactly three dances and he took me back to my table and that was it. He was gone.

One night I was asked to dance by the man who was standing next to me. He was so handsome. He was Italian and he was wearing a white dinner jacket. He was the only man there with a white dinner jacket on. He looked so smart and I go for smartness as well as looks – I want it all! Men have to have clean white teeth, nice clean collars and clean fingernails. I danced with them all, including a male model and a naval officer. I could have bettered myself but I was still getting over Ray. Who would want another man after the life I had led with Ray and the trauma of losing him? Men do like to be macho and dominate women and I had had a lifetime of that. I thought I needed a man like I needed a hole in the head and that I would learn from my mistakes!

The next time Una and I went back to the Mecca, who should be standing just inside the door but a man called Andy. He went to sit at a table with several girls and another man. Una and I bought ourselves a drink and sat at another table. When the music started Andy came and asked me for a dance. He said he was pleased to see me. I couldn't always get out socially and Andy didn't know I had kids. Why would I tell him? I didn't really know him. At the end of the evening Andy walked me home. I left him at St Mary's Church so that he wouldn't know where I lived. I also didn't want to give my nosy neighbours anything to talk about!

Andy and I met several more times at the Mecca. The first time he eventually came to my house he had his best mate with him, who has since died – a young man who drank himself to death. He lived in Scotland and Andy sometimes went up there to the family farm; the family loved Andy.

The first time Andy came to my house alone, there was a pair of Doc Marten boots in the middle of the living room floor. He took one look at the boots and said

'Oh, who wears Doc Marten's?'

'They are my son's and he is 15,' I said.

Andy said he loved Doc Marten's and that his mum never let him have a pair. So that went alright but I thought 'wait until he sees a crowd coming in!' I needn't have worried because it went as right as rain; they all accepted Andy straight away. He was friendly and later on they all went to football together and he also took the little ones sea fishing.

After Andy and I began to see more of each other we went up to Birmingham to meet his mum and dad. Not that we planned to get married or anything like that, Andy just wanted them to meet me. His mother was a bit dubious about our relationship. She said I was very nice but that I was a bit old for Andy. She probably had a point because I was 20 years older than him. He told her that he would go out with who he wanted to and he would marry who he wanted to. His family didn't want anything to do with him while he was living at home with them and they were glad to get him off their hands when he joined the navy. Now here was his mother dictating to him! She never really accepted me but I got on alright with his dad. I did gradually get to know his mum better. She was Welsh and rather a narrow-minded woman.

Andy's dad belonged to a rich family. His dad had polio/infantile paralysis as a child and it left him with one foot shorter than the other. He had his own governess and his own nurse. In his job he became top salesman and he dealt in Irish linens. He visited all the posh hotels and measured up the windows for new curtains – all matching. All the furnishings, the three-piece suites and the chair seats were co-ordinated. It cost the hotels thousands of pounds.

At first Andy's parents lived in a council flat and then they moved into a house. Later they moved to a larger house and then an even bigger house still. Andy's dad couldn't serve in the war because of his polio/infantile paralysis; he didn't pass the medical. He went into the munitions factory instead. Andy's mum also worked in the munitions factory which is where they met and eventually they married. There was a big row because Andy's grandparents didn't want their son to marry a 'nobody'. They said if he married Andy's mum they would cut off his money and that was just what they did!

Towards the end of his life Andy's dad hurt his foot and it became infected so he took to his bed. Andy and I drove to see him and we were told that he had been out of his body twice. That is classed as a dummy run for death; his soul was getting ready to leave his body. The first one frightened him but the second one was a bit scarier. He died in the middle of the night whilst we were visiting him. I was so pleased we went to see him and that he was able to speak to us before he died. I sat and held his hand and Andy's mum looked at me as if she had not seen compassion before. His dad was a gentleman and was very polite and I admired him for that. Eventually, after Andy's mother died, his brother John inherited everything because he had looked after his mother.

Andy and I got married in 1976 at Portsmouth Registry Office while Andy was still in the Royal Navy. He did some time in Ireland but he missed out on a trip to Hong Kong. I so wanted to go to Hong Kong to see the art and culture and learn how to cook their way. I would have loved it. I love sewing and dressmaking as well so it would have suited me down to the ground. Andy was never really liked in the navy so he missed out on a visit to Hong Kong. He was the only man on the ship who went to Belfast in Ireland and because he did that it was classed as an overseas commission. He could have been posted to one of five different overseas postings but his superiors decided he wasn't going to get one and so he didn't. I was more upset about it than he was. It would have been a big adventure for us.

I will always be grateful to Andy because we were able to buy a house together. After having so many kids I thought I would be renting from the council for the rest of my life. Andy is an Aries and he didn't want children, so we never had any. He is the last of his line, so I have been told.

22

Honing my spiritual skills

Both my mum and dad were spiritual. One day, when I was a child and at my nan's house, my mum told me that my dad was in the room. I have always had my own spiritual experiences and as my family grew older and I had more time I wanted to learn more.

Several years ago I saw an advertisement in my local newspaper 'The News' inviting people to join a spiritual seminar at the Joseph Carey Spiritual Foundation. Len Burden was a well-known spiritual/trance medium and clairvoyant in the Portsmouth area for over 50 years. Joseph Carey was Len's main spiritual guide and so Len set up the Joseph Carey Psychic Foundation. I had been to Len for readings several times in the past.

I thought that the course would be interesting and so my daughter and I joined the group. Tony Ashenden, who ran the course, swanned in just like Fred Astaire, the famous dancer. We sat and listened to the talk and enlisted for a course in mediumship and healing, which involved nearly a year's training.

There were 20 of us in the class and the room was packed. Over the weeks and months we were taught how to meditate, how to breathe low from the solar plexus until you almost stopped breathing and were at a point to open up spiritually, as well as many other aspects. The course was quite involved and at the end we had to sit an exam and name all organs of the body, lymph glands and so on. We also had to know about the Chinese and Hindu versions of the body parts.

As the course progressed further we had to sit behind a screen first, then stand up on stage and give psychic readings to the audience.

My second husband, Andy, was in the audience one particular day. When it came to my turn, I stood up and I said I wanted to go to the lady at the back of the room with my message but I couldn't see her face. I said

'There is a gentleman standing next to you and he is reading the newspaper. He was interested in sport. He has a cap on his head rather like the type the horse jockeys wear. He is passing on a message to me. You have a son who plays sport, he plays football. He is asking me to pass this message on to you and you have to warn your son that if he doesn't protect himself properly he will have an accident; an injury that he will never get over and he will never be able to play football again.'

It was a good message. The lady acknowledged me.

We had to give two readings each to members of the audience.

My second reading was for two men who were sitting to the side. I said

'I would like to come to these two gentlemen here.'

I pointed to them; they looked like brothers.

'At the back of you there is a horse in a meadow. It is a beautiful sunny day and the horse is far back in the distance. The horse is on its own and is slowly walking towards me. Can you take this message?'

'No, we don't know anything about a horse' one of them said. I asked them to hold the message because it had a connection with them.

'At the same time there is a gentleman standing behind you in a very dark suit; he looked something like a naval man but he was not in the navy. He was getting on in years; middle-aged and was always on the ships.'

They didn't acknowledge that but thanked me and that was the end of my turn. I felt that I did quite well and passed on exactly what I was shown by spirit.

Later, when we were going home in the car, Andy said to me

'You were having a laugh weren't you, with that woman?'

He carried on driving and I said

'What do you mean?'

'Well, you know who that woman was don't you?'

'How do I know who she was, of course I don't know her.' I didn't even know where she came from; she was just there in front of me in the audience. Andy said

'Her son is a famous footballer. Don't you know who he is?'

'No, I have no idea who he is.'

'He has played for Sheffield United and Southampton' replied Andy.

'Really?'

'Yes, in fact his nickname is Sicknote! He has had so many injuries through football that he is always off sick, hence his nickname.'

My message couldn't have been any better! The gentleman spirit had said that if the footballer did not take the message about his injuries very seriously he would suffer one injury that would never get better.

The message I relayed for the two gentlemen was also accurate. They came to see me in the tea break. They asked if I could tell them any more about the gentleman who was standing beside them. I said

'Well, the feeling that I got was that he was very close to you.' They asked if I could tell them the colour of the buttons on the uniform he was wearing. I said

'They were brass.'

'That was definitely our great-grandfather and the horse belonged to him. He had a farm,' they said to each other.

I was shown the horse in the distance and that meant that the great-grandfather was a long way back in time. So that was how that fitted in with the reading.

At the end of the course we duly received our certificates. Mine are now kept in the attic.

Tony, who ran the course, said to me

'Joan, you won't do platform work; your work will come through your art.'

I was really disappointed because I was looking forward to doing something different. At that time I couldn't possibly see how I would use my art to benefit other people.

Another profound psychic experience happened to me a few years ago at Hayling Island near to my home town. I went there with my daughter. I just went as a spectator because I have drawn and painted many different native American Indians during my life and I wanted to learn more about them. People's faces impress me, no matter what a face looks like. It doesn't have to be a beautiful face; I see something in faces and that's it I have to draw or paint them.

We arrived at a very old thatched house and were shown into the back garden where there was a large tepee. I had to bend down to get in. Inside sat Evandro, a Native American. He was wearing a white shirt; he had white teeth, jet black hair and lights in front of him. He was raised up and he looked quite impressive! I sat on the ground and I remember it was quite cold at that time of year so I couldn't do that too often! There was a tepee pole in the middle and we all sat around in a circle.

Evandro started drumming and then he got up and started walking around us all. He came over to me and I thought 'I am only here because I am curious to learn more about native American Indians.'

Evandro said directly to me

'You get up. You follow me.'

I always seem to get picked on first! He said

'You stand here.'

He left me standing there and he sat down and then the drumming really started. It got a bit louder and a bit louder still and I went into a trance. I could feel myself leading the whole tribe, a multitude of people, and I was lifting up some form of a stave in my hand so that everyone could see it. I started doing a dance.

I could have really impressed them if I had got going! Anyway, after a while the drumming became quieter and I came out of the trance. Evandro said to me

'You my friend, I know you. You know me. I honour you because you led my people to safety.'

That was what I was doing, I was telling them to keep coming, leading them forward.

I didn't know what was happening to me. When a person goes into a trance they are not aware of what they are doing. Someone took photographs of me and they said that my features had totally changed. I was a man, an Indian wearing a bonnet of feathers.

I have been told by a few people that when I have been drawing their spirit guides, I change into different people.

What an experience that was!

23

Finding Peter

Some years ago Janette, my daughter-in-law, sent out a letter of enquiry to try and find my long-lost brother Peter. She made a list of people with the surname of Thomas and she mentioned the Grenadier Guards which Peter had joined and the area we lived in when we were young. Janette became despondent when she had no response from most of the people contacted until, that is, she was due to write to the last few names on the list. She wondered if she should just not bother. The last Thomas on the list lived in a caravan/mobile home and she nearly didn't continue with the task but thought she may as well finish the job and eliminate everyone from the list.

The last reply she received was from my brother Peter! He lived about 40 miles away from me, near Worthing in Sussex. He had come in from work and was in the bath when his wife told him there was a letter from Portsmouth for him. Peter and his wife, Hazel, had been to Portsmouth before and had visited the Isle of Wight. I was living just a few miles away, across The Solent in Portsmouth but of course Peter had no idea whereabouts in the country I was living then.

Peter never tried to get in touch with me in all those years, even when he got married. My mum was at his wedding. Before the wedding Hazel, his future wife, said

'Wouldn't it be nice if we could get Joan to come?'

After all, Peter had visited me some years ago in Guildford when I was in the army and he was in the Grenadier Guards and stationed nearby. We got on well at that time because we were older. So it could have been fairly easy to find me. My mum looked up and replied

'We don't want her here.'

So they never searched for me and I wasn't invited to my own brother's wedding.

My mother was still carrying the past around with her and still calling the shots. What is it I have done to her, or is it something left over from a past life? I have never done her any harm; in fact I worked my fingers to the bone all my early life trying to please her. As a child I used to work in the fields in all weathers. I had bleeding legs and was starving hungry. There were never enough sandwiches made when I was a hungry kid working. I always gave mum the money I earned. I was so proud to give it to her but I never ever got any acknowledgement for it.

So Peter got married and I didn't know about it. I also got married and moved to Portsmouth and Peter didn't know about that either. My mum was still alive and living in Lincoln but I didn't even know whether she was alive or dead. She was still alive when Peter got married and my kids could have had a grand-mother as well as aunts and uncles. I felt really bitter about that for a long time. I felt that my children had missed out on their extended blood family.

Now, many years on, I do not hold any resentment to my family for the way they treated me. That was just how my life was.

Peter Thomas, brother.

Peter and I had been parted for 52 years. The story was in the newspapers. By the time of our reunion Peter and I had aged a lot and were in our sixties. We had a big family get-together; we hired a big hall and had a band playing. It was very strange to meet family we had never seen before.

Some time after the reunion we were at Peter's house one day when the telephone rang. The caller wanted to talk to me. It was a man from a television company. He wanted to put the story of our reunion on TV because it was so long that Peter and I had been separated. I don't know how he had heard about it; someone must have contacted him or overheard about the large reunion being held in the local area. I was speaking to the man on the phone for well over an hour. It would have been quite some story to tell and it would have involved the whole family of course. I was asked a lot of questions and the man said

'This isn't a newspaper story, it's a book!'

'Well, I can't write a book,' I replied.

'No, but I can.'

This was in the 1990s. After all the excitement the story wasn't followed up – I don't know why. The man said he would contact Janette because she was the person who had written the original letter. He wanted to speak to her and arranged to phone her on a particular day at a certain time. The phone wasn't answered – maybe they had had second thoughts. It might have been her husband Graham who stopped her. Graham never liked his dad. He often hid under the bed from him. It could, of course, have been that Peter didn't want our early life exposed publicly.

I don't hold any resentment for my family and their behaviour towards me. My family are no longer alive so I can't hurt them. I was told by Peter, some years later, that my mum died in 1972. Peter suffered from prostate cancer and is no longer alive. Peter's wife tried her hardest to keep the distance between us. She hated it if we were together talking and she interrupted us constantly.

I feel now is the time to share my life story and experiences with others. Not only will it serve as a legacy for my family but I hope it will help other people to live through their own life experiences and difficulties and to know that they are not alone in their suffering. Do as I have had to do, rise like the Phoenix, carry on and *never* give up.

24

Surprise surprise

My family arranged for a surprise 70th birthday party for me in the year 2000. They hired a large room in a local pub, hired a disc jockey and provided a wonderful array of food.

The whole party was a complete surprise to me. Earlier in the day Andy said

'Come on, let's go out for dinner. It's your birthday.'

So I got myself ready and we drove to the pub. When I walked in I was completely overwhelmed. There were so many people there and all of my lovely family and many friends.

My son Steve, the son I had to give away as a baby, was there with his family. I saw him standing there and I just went up to him and put my arms around his neck, in front of everyone. I said to him

'Can you forgive me for what I did?' I sobbed and sobbed, I just couldn't stop crying. He said

'Mum, there is nothing to forgive, I had a great life in Australia and you didn't have much option did you? You did what you thought was right at that terrible time and let me go.'

I had been evicted and had nowhere to go and the authorities threatened to take all of my children away. I felt ashamed that I hadn't been able to bring Steve up as one of mine because I thought he was going to be with Beryl for ever. As he grew into adulthood he began to dislike Beryl for her treatment of him.

Steve is married, has five children and still lives nearby. We see each other as often as we can.

Another complete surprise was that my brother, Peter, and his family were there. It was a huge family get-together, a wonderful birthday surprise and we all had an amazing time.

25

Manifestations

Life was quiet spiritually for a while until I began doing the psychic work that I do now. That was just after the Twin Towers went down in New York on 9th September 2001. I had a serious fire at my house around the same time.

My grandson, Steve, was staying with Andy and me in the house at this time. Steve had a friend called Nigel who was a nice lad, I liked him and we all got on well. In fact it was Nigel who found me my cat, Lily, when she was a kitten. My other cat had just died and Nigel knew I was very upset so he set about finding me another one.

One day Steve had picked me up from my daughter's house and brought me home. Steve said to me

'I was going to have a bath in your house but there was something odd happening in your bathroom.'

He had seen the plant moving and felt an uneasy presence in there. Steve had mentioned this to me on other occasions too. My husband, Andy, had said the same thing but neither of them were spiritual so they didn't believe in spirits. I didn't feel anything in the bathroom and I have had a lifetime of spiritual experiences and am a trained medium. I told them not to worry about it and that I would cleanse the room.

I said

'I tell you what Steve, I will light a candle and put it in the bathroom and I will do an affirmation. I will clear the bathroom and then you can go in and have a bath.'

So I did an affirmation to try and remove any unwanted presence that may have been in there. Steve asked me what he should do with the candle when he had finished in the bathroom. I asked him to put it in my bedroom or leave it in the bathroom and I would deal with it.

Andy hadn't been feeling at all well that day and he was laying down on the floor in the lounge. By then it was about 7 o'clock in the evening when I heard the front door shut. My grandson had gone out saying he would be back in about 20 minutes. I called out

'Ok, make sure you have got your front door key.'

About 10 minutes later I heard a rumpus with lots of noise and banging and Nigel came running into the front room saying

'The house is on fire, quick call the fire brigade!'

Andy had been a fire-fighter in the navy and, even though he was feeling unwell, he jumped up and we rushed to the bottom of the stairs. Steve suddenly appeared at the front door and through the smoke I could just see him running up the stairs with Andy close behind him. I climbed up the stairs and saw a big black void full of thick billowing smoke and they both just disappeared into it. I was coughing and choking and I couldn't believe what was happening! The two kittens we had acquired had to be thrown out of the upstairs window because they had been asleep on my bed. Someone caught them at the bottom. Andy said

'Get out of the house Joan, the house is on fire. That's all I could do to save the kittens. There is nothing we can do; we have called the fire brigade.'

Unluckily our local Fire Station in Copnor had just been closed down due to cutbacks and so the fire fighters had to come from Fareham which was several miles away from us. The fire could have been dealt with much quicker if Copnor fire station had still been operating. My neighbour was very good and took me into her house.

Steve had placed the lighted candle in my bedroom, as I had suggested earlier, and of course it must have melted and fallen over. In my bedroom I had three big bags of material which contained my hand sewing. I had made 12 lovely waistcoats in silk brocade; some were in gold with pretty buttons on them. They were all lined and finished and bagged up ready for Saturday morning because the Joseph Carey Psychic Foundation was going to have a big sale and that was my contribution, as well as a lot of cushions I had made. The firemen tackled the blaze and after the fire was put out I looked around and everything was ruined! I couldn't believe it had happened; it was a devastating and shocking sight. The fire damage was extensive but it was also strange because mostly my things had been burnt; it was as if I was being targeted.

∿

I had to move out of my house for the next four months. That is when I had my second manifestation.

On 11th September 2001 the Twin Towers had gone down in New York. Al-Qaeda terrorists had hi-jacked planes and flown them directly into key buildings in America. The Twin Towers held the World Trade Centre offices and businesses and aeroplanes had been deliberately flown into each of them. It was an unbelievably shocking and distressing event which completely stunned the world. The devastating event is remembered now as 9/11.

At the time I was staying with my daughter while my house was undergoing repairs as a result of the fire. My nine-year-old grandson, Harry, was having nightmares and kept coming downstairs saying

'Nanny, I can't go to sleep. England is going to be bombed and mum and dad are going to be killed and the family is going to be separated.'

'That will never happen darling.' I sat him on my knee and cuddled him. I talked to him and showed him the world and different countries on the globe and the huge distance between England and America. I lay on the bed with him and he went straight off to sleep.

I thought about all the children left without a mum or dad or grandparents and about the awful grief, loss and loneliness they must have felt. It reminded me of my childhood when I was left without my dad and the fear and isolation I constantly felt being alone in the house most of the time.

I felt I wanted to do something to help humanity so I carried out a manifestation. A few days later I went back home to see how my house repairs were progressing. I went into the back room and carried out a manifestation. I asked

'What can I do? What can I do?'

It was really playing on my mind and I thought, wouldn't it be wonderful to say to people 'I can see your guardian angel standing beside you and you don't know they are there because you haven't got a name to call them.' I said

'Look God, you have given me this amazing artistic gift all of my life; I have been able to draw anything I wanted and it has been wonderful; charging bull elephants, racing cars in Monaco, faces, portraits, landscapes – everything. It kept me happy when I was a child for all those hours I was on my own with no one in the house.'

'What can I do? What can I do to pay it all back and help other people?'

Well, I said all of this and I really meant it. I thought it was a good idea. I went back home to Di's house where I was staying.

The following week I returned to my own house again and I said to God

'Look God, I want to get on with this and I haven't heard anything from you yet. Have you had your committee meeting? Don't you think my idea is a good one?'

I said it out loud. I left it at that and I returned to Di's house once again.

At half past four the next morning I awoke and couldn't get back to sleep. I sat up in bed and picked up the book I had been reading 'Channelled' by Alice Bailey. The book was about serving human-ity. There were 12 volumes on the bookshelf in the bedroom and I picked the middle one. I liked the sound of serving humanity and so I started reading the book. After a while I felt that I just had to close my eyes. I left the book open at the page I was reading, closed my eyes and went into a trance. I felt I was flying, just like I had done when I was a child; I was light and floating on air. I was transported into a big white building with high ceilings; it looked like a hospital. Every wall was covered in works of art, all in rows just like an art gallery. I saw one portrait after another, beautiful paintings all close together, with amazing colours and all in heavy gold frames. I was shown a lady sitting on a chair drawing. She didn't say anything but I felt something was being explained to me. I was just amazed. I remember thinking 'What am I doing in an art gallery and why am I here?' I was wearing a long flowing gown and I had someone sitting beside me talking. I couldn't hear what they were saying; I don't think they meant me to hear.

I realised then that I had asked previously to be able to draw portraits of people's guardian angels and spiritual guides and to know their names. I think that the portraits in the frames had been taken from my own paintings and anything that you do which is good in this life is kept and is not destroyed. I believe it is kept because that is part of you for when you move on again into spirit. I came out of the trance and was amazed at how vivid it had been. I felt as though I really was there in that art gallery.

I reached for the book I had been reading. My eyes went straight to the open page and I read 'You will be taken around an art gallery or a university by a spiritual teacher.' I thought Oh my God, that has just happened, it was in my dream/trance. I tried to read the words again on the page but my eyes couldn't find them. Since then, and to this day, I have never seen those words in the book, even though I have searched and searched for them there several times. I thought it was a fluke and so dismissed it out of my mind but it was just the beginning of my next journey. I still wasn't sure what I was going to be doing though.

A few nights later I was in the bedroom and I saw a lady in spirit sitting on the chair. She was a tiny, neat little lady with curly hair. She had a silver aura all around her which shone out against the darkness of the room. I thought I was dreaming and even though I blinked my eyes several times I could still see her. I sat up and composed myself and wondered why was she was there? What did she want? Why was she sitting there like that if she had nothing to say? I came to realise that she was sitting in a pose and wanted her portrait painting. Then she spoke:

'Get on with it then!'

With that she was gone, chair and all and that was it!

I had similar dreams again and realised the message I was being given – that I had to concentrate on the drawing of guardian angels and guides for other people to give them comfort and hope that we live on in spirit.

That was all part of my manifestation. I am proof of the manifestation because I did it, I asked for it and I got it. I manifested from my heart because of all the children and people who suffered as a result of 9/11. The grief and negativity had a lasting and devastating effect all over America and across the world after the disaster.

Sometime later my grandson, Daniel, took me to New York and I saw for myself the utter devastation and chaos; it was absolutely shocking and unbelievable. There was a piece of metal standing like a cross as one memorial of the disaster.

We went into the first church, the one everyone ran into for safety during 9/11, there was a giant Union Jack which covered one wall. In between all the white spaces were the names of each person who had died. I took a picture of the Angel of Light and I placed one of my angel pictures with all the other photographs of the people who had been there and died.

There was complete silence in the church. There were people everywhere paying tribute and I turned around and said to them

'England has full sympathy for you all for what has happened here at this time. We all feel so sad and we all send our support to you.'

I felt that I had to say that to them. I will never forget that and I felt so strongly that I wanted to do something to help others and that is why I manifested for a second time in my life. I say to people now

'You see what I am doing, I am proof that manifestation works and if you want anything then ask from the heart and it will be given.'

26

Drawing on spirits

Eventually I returned to my own home. The repair and re-building work was almost finished and I needed to settle back in. A few days later I had another dream about a lady sitting on a chair by my bed. She looked solid and as if she was posing for a portrait. She said just a few words 'Well, get on with it then!' and suddenly she was gone!

The next day I decided to have a long soak in the bath and I prepared the bathroom. I was lying in the warm water and I must have gone into a trance because I saw the figure of a handsome young man looking at me. He was a native American and he just appeared through my bathroom wall. I quickly finished my bath and I immediately starting drawing his face on my bathroom wall before I forgot what he looked like! Although all the bathroom appliances had been installed, the walls still had to be decorated. I drew him exactly as he had appeared to me. Sometime after that he was covered over when the bathroom was finished. By that time I had drawn him again on paper.

I was apprehensive the first time I did a psychic portrait/reading because I didn't know if I really could do it or how I should go about it. I was told by spirit to get on with it and I need not have worried because it had all been sorted out for me by them.

I went to the next JCPF Psychic Fair and I nervously set up my table with my drawing equipment, artwork and paintings for display. The doors opened at 10 am in the morning and straightaway I had my first customer. I asked the sitter to place her hands onto a large sheet of art paper and I started drawing. I don't remember what I was saying to her. I named her spirit guide and she walked away with her picture. After that I had a steady stream of customers wanting their drawings/readings done. I just about had time for a cup of tea! At around 2 pm one of the organisers said

'Joan, all these people in the queue are waiting to see you.'

Everyone seemed pleased with their drawings and they were talking about it afterwards.

I say to people

'Just place your hands face-down on the paper while I talk and draw.'

Then I place my hands on top of theirs, just for a couple of minutes. When my hands are on top of the sitter's hands I call in Archangel Jophiel and tell him that we are ready. I talk while I am drawing to show that people can see I am not concentrating. I close my eyes and then my hands gradually become hot and then the sitter's hands begin to get hot and then I get pins and needles up my arms. I tell the sitter that is proof we have the Angels with us.

I do channelling beforehand and call in Archangel Jophiel. I ask him three times:

'Archangel Jophiel please will you be with me today? We will work together and it is an honour that I have the pleasure of working with you.'

I absolutely love the work because it makes me laugh as well to think that I have got this giant spiritual being with me. He is very handsome and feminine. He has almost-white hair which is beautiful and he is dressed in green and gold. He is an excellent artist himself. He works with all spiritual artists and gives them his blessing.

I don't hear voices, more a feeling or knowing in my head. Archangel Jophiel puts thoughts into my head. When I call him in he helps bring spirit forward to me. Sometimes I work with other communicators who are Chinese. Some spirits are a bit hesitant about coming forward because they are unsure what will happen. It is rather like going to the dentist for them. The spirits come forward so that I can draw them.

My work has been featured in spiritual magazines. Customers have written to the magazines with their stories of my work and how it has affected their lives. I also have many letters, some from people I have never met, thanking me for their portraits and giving their feedback. Some people telephone me and I give them a reading, others send me paper or a letter on which they have placed their hands and I draw their guardian angel and give a reading from that.

For several years I have been attending psychic fairs and drawing people's guardian angels or spirit guides as well as giving them a name and a psychic reading. I still find it amazing the way it happened for me and I have met some remarkable people through it too. Here are just a few.

My first customer was called Mary. I had an article written about this reading in a magazine. It was circulated widely in Spain and the UK and it resulted in a lot more work for me.

Mary and her boyfriend set up house together. After a while they had an argument and he left her. Mary was frightened living there on her own and she felt that something was happening in the house. She had read a similar story in a magazine and so she contacted me.

I drew Mary's guardian angel for her. I knew she was from Scotland but her guardian angel was Irish. He was called James and he had a brother. James and his brother went to work in the steelworks in Scotland. This was around the early 1900s. James was not very well educated but his brother was. The union movement was being started up at that time. Everyone liked James, he was very popular and had a wonderful character. Because of his charismatic personality he was asked to persuade workers to set-up and join the union. The brothers became well-known in the union and James rose higher in the movement. This was the message I had to pass on to Mary.

Sometime later, after my reading, Mary found a photograph of her and her family standing outside a spooky-looking house and standing with them was her great-grandfather who looked just like James, the man I had drawn for her.

On another occasion I did a drawing and reading for a lady and when I had finished it she told me she didn't know who it was. I apologised that she didn't recognise the person and said that it does happen sometimes but it would come to her in time. She went home with her rolled-up paper with the drawing of her guardian angel on it.

Later, she visited her mother and showed her the drawing of her guardian angel and told her about the reading I had given her. When her mother saw it she nearly fell off her seat! She said

'Oh my God! I can't believe you have got that. That is the young girl I fostered and she died when she was 16. I can't believe that she is with you as your guide. That is wonderful.'

Another drawing I did was of a young man called Luke. He had been in an accident and had passed into spirit. As I was finishing the drawing a lady came over to speak to me. She appeared to be quite emotional and she asked me who I was drawing. I told her that the young man was in spirit as the result of an accident and his name was Luke. The lady told me that he bore a strong resemblance to her own son who had died as a young man in an accident. His name was also Luke.

A few years ago I was working at a local mind, body spirit fair when I met a lady called Dawn who came along with her friend. I was busy drawing and talking to my previous customer and Dawn and her friend stood behind me for some time watching intently what I was doing. They were talking to each other and one of them said

'I don't know. What do you think? Is it real, what she is doing, actually drawing your own guardian angel? Every face she has drawn does look different.' So Dawn said to her friend

'Well, I don't know, I am not sure but she seems to be very busy so there must be something in it.'

Dawn's friend replied

'Well, I have watched her long enough and I am going to have a picture done.'

So she took her turn in the queue and eventually sat at my table. Dawn sat down beside her. It turned out that I drew a picture of her aunt, the aunt who had looked after her in her younger life. When she saw the picture she said

'Oh my God! I can't believe that.'

I asked her why she was so shocked and what was wrong. She replied

'I can't believe it that is my aunt, the lady who helped to bring me up as a child and I really miss her now. I can't believe you have drawn her.'

'Isn't that wonderful, she is still with you in spirit as your guardian angel,' I said.

Another memorable psychic fair was held in a very small hall and it was a squeeze to get all our tables and equipment into the room. One of my sitters turned out to be a man dressed as a woman. We got on very well right from the start. She was tall and used a walking stick due to a previous nasty accident. She had left her partner and she had such an infectious laugh that we laughed all afternoon. I knew it was a man because he had real bright red lipstick on; men often over-do the make-up. She had been in the men's navy but you couldn't mistake the gender because she was so tall.

A lady came through as her guardian angel and it turned out it was one of her relatives. That was one of the best days ever. We laughed so much; everything she said to me made me laugh. Once I start laughing I can't stop but it was lovely and I have seen her at psychic fairs many times since then.

27
Andy's suffering

The first 10 years of mine and Andy's marriage were good; we went on holidays and had a good life. Then Andy came out of the Royal Navy, after Margaret Thatcher said there would be no more promotions and overseas visits for the navy, and he went fishing for nine years. When Andy gets a fixation on something he likes he focuses on nothing else. So off he went fishing and left me at home every weekend. He had the car, he spent the money and went out and enjoyed himself. He didn't seem to care about me. I was up early in the morning cleaning, shopping and cooking, and he came in around eight o'clock in the evening. He didn't really give me a second thought and I changed in that time. I didn't mean to, but life made me change.

Andy was working for Nynex at the time and he began to have difficulty with his co-ordination; loosening and tightening screws became difficult. He went to see his doctor and he was referred to a specialist at the hospital. The specialist thought it could have been a brain tumour but after an x-ray and more tests Andy was told he had the start of Parkinson's disease. At first we couldn't see much change in him but during the next five years, as the disease progressed, he tried to commit suicide twice, he ran away, went missing and was injecting himself with his medication – so he was out of it sometimes.

After suffering for 20 years with Parkinson's Andy had to go into a care home. Occasionally he was lucid mentally but most other times he was confused, irrational and dangerous. The authorities felt he was a risk to himself and to me and the family if he stayed at home. He caused a fire in the kitchen; he wrecked the bathroom in the middle of the night. He soaked everything in the bathroom, took all the towels out of the cupboard, left them on the floor wet and walked out. My neighbour was concerned for my safety when she heard the loud commotion in the night when he was wrecking the bathroom. Another time he put a kettle on the gas hob and nearly started another fire. I came into the kitchen and found a whole four-pint carton of milk all over the floor.

He used to get up in the middle of the night; walk downstairs and out of the front door. Andy also had dementia and in the end it became too dangerous for him to continue living at home.

This is a karma which I must see through and then I may not have to do so much karma in the next life.

The Joseph Carey Psychic Foundation held regular psychic fairs locally. I was at a psychic fair one day and Tony said

'Joan, can I talk to you? I have been given a message and this is what I have to tell you. Can I have a piece of paper and a pencil?'

He drew some lines and curves on the paper and said

'This man has got a really strong jaw, an exceptionally strong jaw. The tunic he is wearing has a piped edging and the collar is not a proper collar but one that stands up, like a Mandarin collar.'

Then he drew the sign of the fish. I said

'Oh, the fish, Pisces.'

Tony and Andy often went fishing together at the time. Tony said

'I know it is not a very good drawing but you will be able to make it good and spirit will help you with it and make sure you get it right.'

'There's the Nile River there.' He drew a line at the back of the man's head and I said 'Egyptian'. He said the name and I never say it properly but it was X e a r t (pronounced Zert).

I took the piece of paper home and I drew this man. His hair was parted in the middle and I drew his features with a very strong jaw-line. I coloured in the drawing, with the Blue Nile, the tunic and piped edging. I felt it was the uniform of some kind of very ancient tribe and I painted the pyramids in the background to show it was Egyptian. Even in my paintings I usually put a clue. I have Archangel

Jophiel with me when I am working; he is a beautiful artist.

Later I said to Tony

'You know Andy is a non-believer in spiritual matters.'

'It's alright this man is going to penetrate Andy's sleep and he will give him healing,' Tony replied.

I understand why Andy is not spiritual because a lot of men aren't. After that I did notice a change in Andy. It took nearly a year but gradually he was smiling a bit more and not dribbling, which was awful because he couldn't control his saliva as a result of the damage to his brain. He had learnt to control that and also I was not continually saying to him

'Andy, I didn't understand a word you said.'

His speech was like a foreign language, all his words rolled out and were slurred; it was difficult to decipher sometimes. There was no real conversation but I had noticed that he seemed to have quietened down a little. He also started walking better and not falling over so much. So he did improve for a time.

Andy eventually went back to the way he was and his illness progressed even further. If Andy didn't want to do a particular thing, he wouldn't do it.

28
Out of body experience

Eight years ago, when I was in my late 70s, I had an out of body experience. A few days earlier I had been feeling unwell and my legs had become swollen. A district nurse came in; she was a very formidable woman, rather like a prison warder. She didn't examine me; she just took one look at my legs, told me I had fluid on my legs and left. The postman could have told me that!

I still felt very unwell a couple of days later and my legs showed no signs of improving so a locum doctor came in to see me. She told me to rest my legs. No one had examined my legs properly or told me what could have caused them to be like that. I wasn't given water tablets because the doctor decided that I would have to go up and downstairs to the bathroom every five minutes if I took those.

Several days later I was still feeling very unwell so I went to bed but I couldn't sleep. I had a very strong gut feeling that if I laid down flat it would kill me. I was in pain and my ribs hurt. I went downstairs, sat in an armchair and didn't move all that night. I felt instinctively that if I moved too much it would be the end of me. I was alright if I sat still and didn't move around at all but as soon as I moved I felt really ill. I learned later that blood clots or embolisms were moving around my body and that was causing me to feel so unwell.

The next day I had been to the bathroom upstairs and as I was walking downstairs I reached the third step and I had another attack. I felt strange, as if I was suffocating and I couldn't breathe. My heart was beating very fast on my left side, under my arm. I climbed back into bed. The same thing happened a short time later. I tried to go downstairs and again I felt exactly the same, as if I was suffocating when I reached the third step. I knew that if I had another attack it would kill me. My daughter called the doctor in. I spoke to the doctor on the phone and she told me that I sounded much worse than on her last visit and she would come around straightaway.

After the doctor examined me she told me to go to the hospital immediately. A friend took me to hospital at six o'clock that evening. I was admitted to the Accident & Emergency Department and I was hooked up to a machine that dispensed heparin. I had had an embolism!

At six o'clock the next morning a male nurse and a sister had just arrived on duty. Everyone else in the ward appeared to be asleep and everything was quiet. I was awake early and I got up to use the toilet which of course happened to be at the other end of the ward! I wondered if I would make it there and back. On my way back to bed I started feeling very strange; my chest felt heavy and I had a choking feeling. The nurse saw me and asked me if I was alright. I tried to lift my hand and say I felt peculiar when suddenly I passed out.

The nurses were nearby and they caught me before I hit the ground. Although I had passed out I seemed to be hovering above the bed. I was looking down watching the two nurses holding me up with their arms around my waist. They were hurrying me along and into the bed. It was just as if I was watching a film. Next I could see the male nurse flapping about and waving his hands around and saying

'Oh my God, she is out of her body, she is out of her body!'

There was absolutely no reading showing on the monitor. I could see the male nurse press the emergency call button and heard the alarm buzzer ringing for help. I watched as more medical staff ran in and the screens were hurriedly closed around my bed. I was hooked up to more monitors. As I looked down at my body I could see that it was black in the middle! That was because I had no soul there; my soul was out of my body. That is what the soul does; it says 'I can't live in this body any more, I have got to go. I could be doing better things.'

After some time they eventually revived me and my daughter Diane was by my side holding my hand. Diane shook my hand and said

'I am here mum; I have got you.'

The doctor was crouching alongside the bed saying

'Hello, hello'.

He was coaxing my spirit back. When I opened my eyes he said

'Hello, oh, you have come back. I am glad you are back.'

I remember looking at the doctor and saying

'What were you doing down there? I was watching you and what was going on.'

A specialist came in to examine me. All the team had come in and the doctor said

'Well you are the celebrity of the day but you put the fear of God into us.'

He said they had never seen anything like it. I had gone stone-cold, like a marble statue. I told the doctor that I wasn't having a heart attack; I felt that my heart was beating under my left arm and it was beating so fast it was stopping me from breathing. If that had gone on it would have killed me. I couldn't breathe, I felt as if someone was strangling me. The doctors told me that they were going to see what was going on inside my body. My blood pressure and oxygen levels had fallen so low the doctor was surprised that I hadn't dropped dead!

I was fast-tracked and hooked up to a heart monitor machine. The doctor prodded my ribs and told me that the reason why my heart felt like it was beating under my left arm was because the left side of my heart was working and the right side was not, hence the irregular/fast heartbeat. My heart was beating alarmingly fast to support the right-hand side. He said that was why I was having an out-of-body experience. Of course, I had been in a bad state for a long time; but I didn't realise that I was so ill. The doctor told me that my heart was enlarged because of the way I had been living. I don't let things put me off; I have such a strong determination and I just carried on. The specialist came in once again and said they had the results of some of the tests but needed to do more tests to see exactly what had been going on. I had a body scan and the monitor showed that I had been living with embolisms for over a year!

I had been doing a lot of spiritual work before this hospital visit. I had been working for the Joseph Carey Psychic Foundation, carrying out healing and giving out my energy which made me feel ill the next day. I couldn't understand why I was feeling so bad because I should have been feeling really good. I didn't realise I had embolisms in my body. The specialist told me that one side of my heart was doing all the work and that is why my body had had enough. Your soul can leave the body. It was a hard trek back and I remember thinking about my family and how it would shake them up.

When the doctor next came in I had been trying to write out a postcard to my brother because he had prostate cancer. The doctor held my arm and said

'You are ill and here you are, thinking about your brother.'

What else would I want to do? Everybody came to see me, everyone who had heard about it in the hospital, and I said

'Thank you for all you have done for me.'

'No, we should be thanking you for the sensation you have caused here. We have never had such an experience and it has all gone down on record,' the doctor replied.

Patients are not supposed to stay in the medical emergency ward for more than 24 hours but I was there for a week because they were waiting to see if I was going to have another attack. My wonderful family looked after me well, with lots of food and tea. I am truly blessed, I was wrapped up in sheets of gold by my family.

I was in a bed at the end of the ward in the corner and the woman opposite me said

'I am not even going to look at you, because I am supposed to be here recovering from a heart attack and you are making me laugh.'

I do like to see a smile on people's faces; I hate to see people upset. One of my old customers was brought into the ward during the night and the next morning I awoke to see him in the bed opposite me.

I said

'Oh look, it's Roy over there.'

He had been into hospital several times before and his wife had died some time ago. I had painted three different pictures for him and a portrait of his guardian angel after his wife had died. He told me he had seen his wife and she was looking at him. He said she appeared in a lot of gold clouds and her face appeared in the middle. She told him to go and comfort other people. So Roy often went to the cemetery and if he saw someone who was sad or upset he went and talked to them. He was a lovely man and he had one daughter.

When he saw me there in the same ward he said

'Oh my God, I can't believe it, it's Joan Smee!'

His daughter was sitting on the bed and she turned round, looked at me and said

'I can't believe it. I asked for someone to be there to comfort my dad and there you are! My father is in such awe of you.'

They were wonderful words.

29

Wonder Women

In 2014 I was invited to give a talk to a local group called Wonder Women at a school near to where I once lived, in Leigh Park. One of my customers from years before, Dawn, belonged to this group of women who 'wonder about everything' and different speakers were invited to come and talk to the group. Dawn had suggested that I should be asked to come and talk about my life.

Everyone came into the room and settled down. The organiser, Chris, introduced me and said

'Well, Joan, the floor is yours now.'

I had been thinking about what I was going to say while everyone was sitting down. I had a glass of water and I was turning the glass round and thinking 'Where am I going to start?' So I thought I would start with the time when the Twin Towers came down in America and the profound effect it had on me.

Everyone sat in silence, waiting for me to speak. I thought then that I really needed to start at the beginning of my life, whether they liked it or not. I started talking about my dad when he was alive and looking after me and I was a small tot, and lying in bed near the fire because I had bronchitis. Well it was always my dad who looked after me. My mum never came anywhere near me, she didn't even come downstairs.

Then I told them about my dad committing suicide and me being left on my own at four years old. I have it all recorded on my family tree. I also told them about me trying to climb up the trestle because my dad was in a coffin and was going to be buried. People stayed in their own home in those days and all the relatives and friends would come and say their goodbyes to the departed and offer condolences to the family. My mum didn't comfort me or tell me what was happening or lift me up to see my dad, there was never any tenderness. She just didn't want me.

I am sorry but that is how I feel, it has affected me the whole of my life. The whole issue lived with me and followed me around – and it still does. It is more in the past now but because I am recalling the story it affects me less now. I have got to cold shoulder everything, that's how I deal with it. I always pick myself up and dust myself down, no matter what I have to face the next day. I like my life now and all those experiences have made me a stronger person.

I carried on talking about my life and when it came to the tea break I looked around the room and everyone was so quiet; you could have heard a pin drop.

I was invited back a second time, some weeks later, to continue my story and answer a lot of questions. I have made some genuine friends from those visits – and that is how I came to write about my life.

Joan at Work: Mind, Body and Spirit Fairs.

Geronimo – Native American Indian Chief of the Apache Tribe

Drawing of Dawn's Guardian Angel/Spirit Guide. Her name is simply 'She' and the bird guides her to help animals find food in the Winter. She wears a necklace of prayer knots.

Native American Indian – A vision drawn on Joan's bathroom wall and later a painting.

Laughing Cavalier, painted around 1965.

Elegant lady with small dog, painted in 2016.

Paramahamsa Swami Vishwananda,
enlightened spiritual master.

Buddha – Buddha of protection of small children.
Painted from a 13 metre statue in Japan.

Gaia's Abundance – Mother Earth

Zara the Snow Goddess
*Zara protects all small creatures and guides them to food in
cold weather.*

A sketch of me as a girl sitting at a wooden tea-chest table in the back garden drawing. The big dark tree which Peter and I often climbed is to the side.
I am alone – but not quite alone!
This is just how I remember it.

30
Laying down foundations

When I reflect back on my lifetime I feel satisfied that, although I had a difficult beginning and much of my following life was full of a long series of mostly bad experiences, I see my children, grandchildren and now great-grandchildren and I realise that my skills are being carried on by them. They are good and kind people with many talents – music, art and sewing amongst others. I know why I had to live my life as it unfolded, to pass on to future generations the lessons I have had to learn and the many experiences I have lived through.

So many times I could have succumbed to self-pity or depression. I could have raised my children the same way as I had been brought up, unloved and unwanted as I was for most of my childhood. I could have repeated my own early life and chosen to not teach them the ways of the world but instead I decided to live my life for them and teach them the lessons I had to learn the hard way throughout my life. I have never felt resentful. I have been hurt and humiliated and I have cried a lot of tears but I am not vicious; it is not in my nature. People have asked me many times why I didn't seek revenge but there is a saying in my family 'every dog has its day.' I truly believe that, and my daughter made me a cushion with a dog and that saying on it – just to remind me!

I have had to learn many lessons throughout my life but it has all been worthwhile. I have had no choice but to carry on and deal with these difficult experiences myself. My own personality has helped me immensely and my faith has kept me going. I hope I have worked off a lot of karma in this lifetime. I would say to everyone: never give up, rise up like the Phoenix and carry on. These may be easy words to say but really the alternative doesn't bear thinking about.

Now I am in my 80s and over a year ago I fell and broke my pelvis in two places! I have been recovering from yet another terrible experience but it is the love and wonderful care of my family which has helped me through. I am still doing my work at the mind, body and spirit psychic fairs and I still do readings and drawings at my home for customers who contact me. As well as my psychic work I am still drawing and painting and I am currently working on different painting commissions as well as organising prints of my work. My work has won competitions and it has also been featured in magazines.

Oh yes, and I am also writing a book about my life! My autobiography has been suggested several times in the past, by people who are intrigued by my experiences, and now it is time to share my story. After all, I may not get another chance!

If I can help others who have suffered these experiences or have been in similar situations to me to cope with their problems then writing about my life will have been worthwhile. I do wonder what else is in store for me...?

Acknowledgements

My thanks to my amazing and talented family of whom I am so proud and for sharing my story.

I am grateful to my many friends and acquaintances for being a part of my life and to all those who have contributed towards my final book. Thanks also to Viv Clarke for the many hours patiently spent transcribing my memoirs and for the shared friendship, laughter and tears during the process.

I would also like to thank Anne and Mark Webb at Paragon Publishing for their help in editing and publishing this book.

About the Author

Joan Louise Smee was born in 1930 in the industrial north of England. She is an accomplished and acclaimed artist and psychic and continues to paint and work, giving messages and guidance to people through her drawings.
A mother, grandmother and great-grandmother, Joan lives in Portsmouth, England.

E-mail: phoenixlife3019@gmail.com